BEGINNERS MUSHROOM CULTIVATION

A Comprehensive Mushroom Cultivation Guide

Joseph C. Owens

Beginners Mushroom Cultivation

TABLE OF CONTENT

Walter K. Byrne

PREFACE

Welcome to "BEGINNERS MUSHROOM CULTIVATION: A Comprehensive Mushroom Cultivation Guide"! I'm thrilled to embark on this fungal journey with you.

If you're holding this book, chances are you share my passion for mushrooms. Whether you're a curious beginner or an aspiring mycologist, this guide is designed to be your trusty companion on the path to cultivating your own fungi.

Mushroom cultivation might seem daunting at first glance, but fear not! I remember the excitement and uncertainty I felt when I started my own mushroom cultivation journey. That's why I've written this book—to demystify the process and empower you with the knowledge and confidence to grow your own delicious mushrooms right at home.

In these pages, you'll find a comprehensive exploration of mushroom cultivation, from understanding the basics to mastering advanced techniques. We'll cover everything from selecting the right mushroom species and setting up your cultivation space to troubleshooting common issues and harvesting your bountiful crops.

But this book is more than just a manual—it's a celebration of the incredible world of fungi. From the humble button mushroom to exotic varieties like lion's mane and oyster mushrooms, we'll dive into the fascinating diversity of mushrooms and their culinary delights.

I've poured my heart and soul into crafting this guide, drawing from years of personal experience and the expertise of fellow mushroom enthusiasts. My hope is that it will not only equip you with practical skills but also inspire a deeper appreciation for the wonders of mushroom cultivation.

So, whether you're dreaming of homegrown shiitakes or eager to explore the cutting edge of mycological innovation, grab your trowel and let's get growing!

CHAPTER 1

Introduction to Mushroom Cultivation

So, why mushrooms? Well, let me tell you—they're more than just tasty additions to your favorite dishes. Mushrooms are nature's recyclers, breaking down organic matter and returning nutrients to the soil. Plus, they're packed with flavor, nutrition, and medicinal properties, making them a valuable addition to any kitchen or medicine cabinet.

But before we dive into the nitty-gritty of cultivation, let's take a step back and marvel at the rich history of mushroom cultivation. Did you know that humans have been cultivating mushrooms for thousands of years? From ancient civilizations to modern-day mushroom farms, the art of mushroom cultivation has evolved and flourished across cultures and continents.

Now, you might be wondering—what exactly is mushroom cultivation? At its core, mushroom cultivation is the intentional growing of mushrooms for food, medicine, or other purposes. Unlike plants, mushrooms don't grow from seeds. Instead, they propagate through spores, which are microscopic reproductive cells found in the gills or pores of mature mushrooms.

In the wild, mushrooms thrive in diverse ecosystems, from lush forests to decaying logs. But with the right knowledge and techniques, you can recreate these natural conditions right in your own home or backyard. That's the beauty of mushroom cultivation—you don't need a green thumb or acres of land to get started. With a little patience and ingenuity, anyone can grow their own mushrooms, regardless of their experience level or background.

Throughout this book, we'll explore the ins and outs of mushroom cultivation, from selecting the right mushroom species to harvesting your first flush of mushrooms. Whether you're a seasoned gardener or a complete novice, I'm confident that you'll find something valuable in these pages to ignite your passion for mushroom cultivation.

Understanding the Basics

First things first—let's talk about what mushrooms actually are. Contrary to popular belief, mushrooms aren't plants; they belong to their own unique kingdom called fungi. Fungi play a vital role in ecosystems around the world, breaking down organic matter and recycling nutrients. And mushrooms? Well, they're just the tip of the fungal iceberg—a small, visible part of a much larger and often invisible network of mycelium, the fungal equivalent of roots.

Now, when it comes to cultivating mushrooms, there are a few key factors to consider, the most important of which is substrate. Think of substrate as the food source for your mushrooms—it's what they'll feed on as they grow. Substrates can take many forms, from straw and sawdust to coffee grounds and even cardboard. Each mushroom species has its own preferred substrate, so it's essential to choose the right one for the mushrooms you want to grow.

Next up, let's talk about growing conditions. Mushrooms are picky little creatures when it comes to their environment, so creating the perfect conditions for them to thrive is crucial. Temperature, humidity, and light are all factors to consider, as they can vary depending on the species of mushroom you're growing. Some mushrooms prefer cooler temperatures and high humidity, while others thrive in warmer, drier conditions.

In addition to environmental factors, timing is also important in mushroom cultivation. Mushrooms have a life cycle just like any other living organism, and understanding the stages of their growth is key to successfully cultivating them. From inoculation to fruiting, each stage requires careful attention and management to ensure a bountiful harvest.

Mushroom cultivation is a practice in patience and perseverance. Unlike many plants, mushrooms don't sprout overnight. It can take weeks or even months for your mushrooms to mature, so don't be discouraged if you don't see results right away. With time, care, and a little bit of luck, your efforts will be rewarded with a beautiful crop of delicious, homegrown mushrooms.

So, there you have it—the basics of mushroom cultivation laid out before you. With this knowledge, you're well on your way to becoming a successful mushroom cultivator. In the chapters that follow, we'll dive deeper into the specific techniques and methods you'll need to know to bring your mushroom-growing dreams to life. So, stay curious, stay patient, and most importantly, have fun!

Why Cultivate Mushrooms?

Why cultivate mushrooms? Allow me to shed some light on this delightful topic as we explore the myriad reasons why growing mushrooms is not just a hobby, but a deeply rewarding and enriching experience.

First and foremost, let's talk about flavor. If you've ever tasted a freshly harvested mushroom—whether it's the earthy richness of a portobello or the delicate sweetness of a shiitake—you'll know that store-bought mushrooms simply can't compare. When you grow your own mushrooms, you have complete control over their quality and freshness, resulting in a culinary experience that's truly unparalleled.

But mushrooms are so much more than just a feast for the taste buds—they're also nutritional powerhouses, packed with vitamins, minerals, and antioxidants. From immune-boosting shiitakes to brain-boosting lion's mane, each mushroom variety offers its own unique health benefits, making them a valuable addition to any diet.

Beyond their culinary and nutritional value, mushrooms also have a fascinating array of medicinal properties. For centuries, mushrooms have been used in traditional medicine systems around the world to treat a wide range of ailments, from immune disorders to cardiovascular disease. And with modern scientific research increasingly validating these ancient practices, the medicinal potential of mushrooms is only beginning to be fully understood.

But perhaps the most compelling reason to cultivate mushrooms is their environmental impact. Unlike traditional crops, which require large amounts of land, water, and resources to grow, mushrooms can be cultivated using minimal space and inputs. Plus, mushrooms are natural recyclers, breaking down organic matter and returning nutrients to the soil, making them a sustainable and eco-friendly choice for conscientious growers.

Last but not least, let's talk about the sheer joy of growing mushrooms. There's something truly magical about watching a tiny spore transform into a bountiful harvest of delicious mushrooms right before your eyes. Whether you're a seasoned gardener or a complete novice, the process of nurturing mushrooms from start to finish is a deeply satisfying and fulfilling experience that connects you to the rhythms of nature in a profound way.

So, why cultivate mushrooms? The real question is—why not? With their incredible flavor, nutritional benefits, medicinal properties, environmental sustainability, and sheer joy of growing, mushrooms offer a wealth of reasons to dive headfirst into the world of mushroom cultivation. So, what are you waiting for?

Brief History of Mushroom Cultivation

Our story begins in ancient times, where mushrooms held a place of reverence and mystery in cultures around the world. From the sacred rituals of indigenous peoples to the royal feasts of emperors, mushrooms were prized for their medicinal, culinary, and even spiritual properties. In ancient China, for example, mushrooms were believed to bestow immortality, while in ancient Egypt, they were considered a food fit for pharaohs.

In the Middle Ages, mushrooms were still shrouded in myth and superstition. In Europe, mushrooms were associated with witches and witchcraft, leading to fear and suspicion among the general populace. Yet, despite these fears, mushrooms continued to play a vital role in medieval medicine and cuisine, with monks and herbalists alike extolling their virtues.

It wasn't until the Renaissance that mushrooms began to emerge from the shadows and take their rightful place in the culinary spotlight. In 17th century France, the cultivation of mushrooms began in earnest, with the discovery of the champignon de Paris, or button mushroom, in the underground quarries of Paris. This humble fungus would soon become the cornerstone of modern mushroom cultivation, paving the way for the mass production of mushrooms on an industrial scale.

In the centuries that followed, mushroom cultivation continued to evolve and expand, with new varieties being discovered and cultivated around the world. From the exotic enoki mushrooms of Japan to the savory porcini mushrooms of Italy, each culture has put its own unique spin on mushroom cultivation, resulting in a diverse and vibrant tapestry of fungal delights.

As trade routes expanded, mushrooms cut across continents, enriching cultures and cuisines along the way. In Asia, mushrooms played a central role in traditional medicine and cuisine for millennia. Ancient texts from China and India extolled the medicinal virtues of mushrooms, prescribing them for everything from longevity to vitality.

Meanwhile, in Europe, mushrooms continued to inspire both awe and apprehension. During the Age of Exploration, European explorers encountered new varieties of mushrooms in the New World, including the prized morel and chanterelle mushrooms. These exotic fungi captivated the palates of European nobility, leading to a surge in demand for imported mushrooms and sparking a culinary craze that swept across the continent.

In the 19th century, the art and science of mushroom cultivation took a giant leap forward with the discovery of the mushroom's life cycle. Scientists like Louis Pasteur and Anton de Bary revolutionized our understanding of fungi, laying the groundwork for modern mycology. Meanwhile, entrepreneurs like William Robinson and Charles McIlvaine pioneered innovative techniques for cultivating mushrooms on an industrial scale, transforming mushroom cultivation from a cottage industry into a thriving commercial enterprise.

By the 20th century, mushroom cultivation had become a global phenomenon, with mushrooms being grown and consumed on every continent. Advances in technology, such as the invention of the mushroom composting process and the development of controlled environment growing chambers, revolutionized mushroom cultivation, making it more efficient and sustainable than ever before.

Today, mushroom cultivation is more popular and accessible than ever before, thanks to advances in technology and a growing interest in sustainable living. Whether you're a hobbyist growing mushrooms in your backyard or a commercial farmer producing mushrooms for market, the possibilities are endless.

Reflecting on the remarkable journey of mushroom cultivation, let us marvel at the ingenuity and resilience of humankind—and of fungi themselves. For in the humble mushroom, we find not only a source of sustenance and delight but also a symbol of our enduring connection to the natural world.

Type of Mushrooms

Button Mushroom

Button Mushroom

First, we have the classic champignon de Paris, also known as the button mushroom. Despite its unassuming appearance, the button mushroom boasts a rich history and a wide range of culinary applications. Originally cultivated in the underground quarries of Paris in the 17th century, the button mushroom has since become the most widely cultivated mushroom globally.

What sets the button mushroom apart is its mild, earthy flavor and firm, meaty texture. These versatile fungi are equally at home in soups, salads, stir-fries, and sauces, making them a staple ingredient in kitchens worldwide. Whether sliced raw in salads, sautéed with garlic and herbs, or stuffed and baked to perfection, the button mushroom's versatility knows no bounds.

shiitake mushrooms

Next, let's talk about shiitake mushrooms, beloved for their rich, savory flavor and meaty texture. Originating in East Asia, particularly Japan and China, shiitake mushrooms have been cultivated for thousands of years and are prized for their umami-rich taste and meaty texture.

shiitake mushrooms

What sets shiitake mushrooms apart is their distinctive flavor profile, which is often described as savory, earthy, and slightly smoky. These hearty fungi are beloved for their ability to add depth and complexity to a wide range of dishes, from soups and stews to stir-fries and sushi. Rich in essential nutrients and bioactive compounds, shiitake mushrooms are also valued for their potential health benefits, including immune support and cholesterol management.

Shiitake mushrooms have a long history of use in traditional medicine, where they're believed to promote longevity, vitality, and overall well-being. Today, shiitake mushrooms are enjoyed both for their culinary delights and their potential health benefits, making them a cherished ingredient in kitchens and medicine cabinets alike.

Oyster Mushrooms

The delicate elegance of oyster mushrooms, named for their resemblance to oysters, comes in a variety of colors, including creamy white, pink, yellow, and blue. With their delicate, velvety caps and tender, juicy texture, oyster mushrooms are prized for their subtle sweetness and earthy aroma. What sets oyster mushrooms apart is their versatility in the kitchen. Whether sautéed, stir-fried, grilled, or roasted, oyster mushrooms add a delightful depth of flavor and texture to a wide range of dishes. From creamy risottos and hearty pastas to flavorful stir-fries and savory soups, there's no shortage of creative ways to enjoy these elegant fungi. Oyster mushrooms are also valued for their nutritional benefits. Low in calories and fat, yet rich in protein, fiber, and essential nutrients like vitamin D and B vitamins, oyster mushrooms are a healthy and nutritious addition to any diet. Plus, they're a natural source of antioxidants and bioactive compounds, making them a valuable ally in supporting overall health and well-being.

Portobello Mushrooms

Portobello Mushrooms

Portobello mushrooms, known for their robust flavor and meaty texture, portobello mushrooms are the mature form of the button mushroom, harvested when fully grown. With their large, flat caps and dense, chewy texture, portobello mushrooms are often compared to steak, making them a popular choice for vegetarian and vegan dishes. What sets portobello mushrooms apart is their versatility in the kitchen. Whether grilled, roasted, stuffed, or used as a meat substitute in burgers and sandwiches, portobello mushrooms add a rich, savory depth to any dish. With their umami-rich flavor and satisfying texture, portobello mushrooms are a favorite among carnivores and herbivores alike. Portobello mushrooms are also valued for their nutritional benefits. Low in calories and fat, yet rich in protein, fiber, and essential nutrients like potassium and selenium, portobello mushrooms are a nutritious and delicious addition to any meal. Plus, they're a natural source of antioxidants and bioactive compounds, making them a valuable ally in supporting overall health and wellness.

Enoki mushrooms

Enoki mushrooms, also known as golden needle mushrooms or enokitake, are prized for their delicate appearance and mild, slightly fruity flavor. With their long, thin stems and tiny, button-like caps, enoki mushrooms resemble delicate strands of golden thread, making them a visually striking addition to any dish. What sets enoki mushrooms apart is their versatility in the kitchen. Whether enjoyed raw in salads, added to soups and stir-fries, or used as a garnish for sushi and noodle dishes, enoki mushrooms add a delightful crunch and subtle sweetness to a wide range of culinary creations. Plus, their delicate texture and mild flavor make them a favorite among both novice and experienced cooks alike. Enoki mushrooms are valued for their potential health benefits. Rich in essential nutrients like B vitamins, potassium, and antioxidants, enoki mushrooms are believed to support immune function, promote heart health, and aid in digestion. Plus, they're a low-calorie, low-fat source of protein and fiber, making them a nutritious and delicious addition to any diet.

Lion's Mane Mushrooms

Lion's mane mushrooms, named for their striking resemblance to the flowing mane of a lion, these unique fungi are prized for their distinctive appearance and rich, savory flavor. With their cascading, waterfall-like tendrils and snowy white color, lion's mane mushrooms are a visually stunning addition to any dish. What sets lion's mane mushrooms apart is their unique texture and flavor profile. Unlike most mushrooms, which have a meaty or chewy texture, lion's mane mushrooms have a delicate, almost fluffy texture that melts in your mouth. And their flavor? Think of a cross between lobster and crab—rich, savory, and slightly sweet, with hints of umami and buttery goodness.

Lion's mane mushrooms are valued for their potential health benefits. Rich in bioactive compounds like polysaccharides and hericenones, lion's mane mushrooms are believed to support cognitive function, promote nerve regeneration, and reduce inflammation. Plus, they're a natural source of antioxidants and antimicrobial compounds, making them a valuable ally in supporting overall health and wellness.

But the world of mushrooms goes far beyond these popular types. There are hundreds, if not thousands, of mushroom species waiting to be explored, each with its own unique flavor, texture, and potential. So, whether you're a seasoned mushroom aficionado or a curious beginner, I encourage you to explore the diverse and wonderful world of mushrooms. With so many varieties to choose from, there's always something new and exciting to try. Happy mushroom hunting, my fellow fungi enthusiasts!

CHAPTER 2

Getting Started

Alright, my fellow mushroom enthusiast, it's time to roll up our sleeves and dive into the exciting world of mushroom cultivation! In this chapter, I'll guide you through the essential steps to get started on your mushroom-growing journey, from selecting the right mushroom species to setting up your cultivation space.

Selecting the Right Mushroom Species

Let's embark on the exciting journey of selecting the perfect mushroom species for your cultivation project! With so many varieties to choose from, it can feel a bit overwhelming at first, but fear not—I'm here to help you navigate the wonderful world of mushrooms and find the perfect match for your growing goals.

First things first, let's consider your level of experience and comfort with mushroom cultivation. If you're new to growing mushrooms, you'll want to start with species that are known for being beginner-friendly and forgiving of mistakes. Trust me, we all make them in the beginning! Some great options for beginners include the classic button mushroom (Agaricus bisporus) and the versatile oyster mushroom (Pleurotus spp.). These varieties are relatively easy to grow and produce consistent yields, making them perfect for novice cultivators.

On the other hand, if you're feeling a bit more adventurous and want to try your hand at growing something a bit more exotic, there are plenty of exciting options to choose from. How about the earthy and aromatic shiitake mushroom (Lentinula edodes), prized for its rich flavor and medicinal properties? Or perhaps the striking lion's mane mushroom (Hericium erinaceus), with its unique appearance and delicate texture? These varieties may require a bit more care and attention, but the rewards are well worth the effort.

Next, let's consider your growing environment and available resources. Some mushroom species thrive in specific conditions, such as temperature, humidity, and light levels, so it's important to choose a species that's well-suited to your particular setup. For example, if you have limited space or are growing indoors, you'll want to choose species that can tolerate lower light levels and are well-suited to container or bag cultivation.

One of the best parts of growing your own mushrooms is getting to enjoy the delicious fruits of your labor! Consider the flavor, texture, and culinary versatility of each mushroom species, and choose varieties that align with your taste preferences and cooking style. Whether you prefer the meaty texture of portobello mushrooms or the delicate flavor of enoki mushrooms, there's a mushroom out there to suit every palate.

So there you have it—your guide to selecting the right mushroom species for your cultivation project!

Setting Up Your Cultivation Space

Now, let's find the ideal location for our mushroom-growing endeavors. Whether you're growing indoors or outdoors, you'll want to choose a clean, well-lit space with stable temperature and humidity levels. Ideally, your cultivation space should be between 60-75°F (15-24°C) and have humidity levels of 80-90%.

If you're growing indoors, consider setting up in a spare room, closet, basement, or garage—anywhere that's clean, relatively quiet, and easily accessible.

Keeping your cultivation space clean and free from contaminants is essential for preventing mold, bacteria, and other harmful organisms from interfering with your mushroom growth. Be sure to clean and disinfect your containers, tools, and work surfaces regularly, and practice good hygiene practices like washing your hands before handling mushrooms or working in your cultivation space.

Ventilation is also important for ensuring a healthy growing environment for your mushrooms. Proper air circulation helps prevent the buildup of carbon dioxide and excess moisture, which can lead to mold and other problems. If you're growing indoors, consider using fans or vents to promote air exchange, and be sure to monitor temperature and humidity levels regularly to ensure they remain within the optimal range.

Whether you're growing in containers or bags, it's important to arrange your cultivation space in a way that maximizes efficiency and accessibility. Arrange your containers or bags in a single layer to ensure even airflow and light distribution, and leave enough space between them to allow for easy access and maintenance. Keep your tools, materials, and equipment organized and within reach, and consider setting up a dedicated work area for preparing substrates, inoculating spawn, and monitoring mushroom growth.

By carefully considering these factors and setting up your cultivation space with care and attention to detail, you'll create the perfect environment for growing healthy, bountiful mushrooms. So take your time, plan ahead, and get ready to enjoy the fruits of your labor as you embark on your mushroom-growing journey!

Equipment and Materials Overview

Here's what you'll need:

Growing Bags

Containers or growing bags: Choose containers or bags that are suitable for the type of mushrooms you're growing and the substrate you'll be using. Plastic or glass containers work well for indoor cultivation, while breathable fabric bags are ideal for outdoor cultivation.

Substrate: Select a suitable substrate for your chosen mushroom species. This could be anything from straw and sawdust to coffee grounds and cardboard. Be sure to choose a substrate that's clean, free from contaminants, and well-suited to the needs of your mushrooms.

Mushroom spawn: This is the fungal equivalent of seeds, and it's what you'll use to inoculate your substrate and kickstart the growth process. You can purchase mushroom spawn from specialty suppliers or online retailers, or you can make your own using a mushroom culture or spores.

Other equipment: Depending on your setup, you may also need things like a pressure cooker or steamer for sterilizing your substrate, a thermometer and hygrometer for monitoring temperature and humidity levels, and a spray bottle for misting your mushrooms.

Once you have everything you need, it's time to set up your cultivation space. Start by cleaning and disinfecting your containers or bags to prevent contamination. If you're growing indoors, consider laying down a clean, sterile surface like a plastic sheet or tarp to work on.

Next, prepare your substrate according to the instructions for your chosen mushroom species. This may involve sterilizing the substrate to kill off any potential contaminants and create a clean, hospitable environment for your mushrooms to grow.

Once your substrate is prepared, it's time to inoculate it with mushroom spawn. Depending on the type of substrate and spawn you're using, this process may involve mixing the spawn into the substrate by hand, layering it between substrate layers, or injecting it into the substrate using a syringe or pipette.

After inoculation, place your containers or bags in your cultivation space and monitor them carefully for signs of growth. Depending on the mushroom species and growing conditions, it can take anywhere from a few weeks to several months for your mushrooms to mature, so be patient and don't be discouraged if you don't see results right away.

CHAPTER 3

Where to Grow Mushroom

Choosing the right spot is crucial for creating the ideal environment for your mushrooms to grow. Whether you have a spacious garden or a cozy apartment, there's a perfect place for your mushroom cultivation. Let's explore the possibilities together.

Indoor Growing

If you're growing mushrooms indoors, you have the advantage of controlling the environment more precisely. Here are some great indoor options:

Spare Room or Closet: A spare room or a large closet can be transformed into a perfect mushroom-growing space. Just make sure it's clean and can be kept at a stable temperature and humidity level. You need to clean the area thoroughly to eliminate any potential contaminants. Wipe down surfaces with a mild bleach solution or alcohol. Install sturdy, adjustable shelves to maximize your growing area. Make sure the shelves can support the weight of your containers or bags filled with substrate and mushrooms. Mushrooms don't require intense light but do benefit from some indirect light. You can use fluorescent or LED grow lights set to a 12-hour on/off cycle to mimic natural light conditions. Use a humidifier to maintain humidity levels between 80-90%. A hygrometer will help you monitor and adjust humidity as needed. You might also want to mist the air regularly with a spray bottle.

Basement: Basements are naturally cooler and darker, which can be beneficial for mushroom growth. Ensure proper air circulation using fans to prevent stagnant air and mold growth. You might need a dehumidifier if your basement is too damp.

Use space heaters or coolers to maintain the optimal temperature range. Basements can sometimes get too cold, so keep an eye on the thermometer. Similar to the spare room setup, install shelves and use grow lights if your basement doesn't get natural light.

Garage: Garages can be a versatile space for mushroom cultivation. If your garage isn't insulated, consider adding insulation to help regulate temperature. Similar to basements, use heaters, coolers, and humidifiers to create the ideal environment. Since garages can be dusty or dirty, keep your cultivation area isolated from other activities and regularly clean the space.

Grow Tents: Grow tents are perfect for creating a controlled environment in a limited space.

Choose a grow tent that fits your available space. They often come with built-in ventilation ports, reflective interiors, and light fixtures. Use the provided ports for wiring grow lights and setting up humidifiers. Tents help maintain high humidity levels naturally due to their enclosed design. Ensure proper airflow with small fans or the tent's built-in ventilation system to prevent mold and promote healthy mushroom growth.

Outdoor Growing

Shaded Garden Area

An outdoor garden offers a natural environment for mushroom cultivation.

- **Location**: Choose a spot with dappled sunlight, such as under trees or next to a north-facing wall. This prevents mushrooms from getting too much direct sunlight, which can dry them out.
- **Substrate Beds**: Prepare substrate beds directly on the ground. Use a mixture of organic materials like straw, wood chips, or compost, depending on your mushroom species.
- **Moisture Management**: Keep the substrate moist by watering regularly, but avoid waterlogging. You can cover the substrate with a breathable material like burlap to retain moisture.

Patio or Porch

A covered patio or porch can provide a sheltered environment for your mushrooms. Use containers or grow bags placed on shelves or directly on the floor. Ensure they're in a spot with indirect sunlight. Use a tarp or shade cloth to protect your setup from heavy rain or strong winds. This helps maintain stable moisture levels and prevents contamination. Water the substrate as needed to keep it moist. Misting systems can be set up for consistent moisture.

Log Cultivation

Cultivating mushrooms on logs is a more traditional method.

- Choose hardwood logs like oak, maple, or birch, which are suitable for species like shiitake and oyster mushrooms. The logs should be freshly cut and free from rot.
- Drill holes in the logs and fill them with mushroom spawn. Seal the holes with wax to protect the spawn and retain moisture.
- Place the inoculated logs in a shaded, moist area. Stand them upright or lay them horizontally on the ground.
- Water the logs during dry periods to maintain moisture. Logs can take several months to a year to start producing

mushrooms, but once they do, they can produce for several years.

Additional Tips for Any Growing Location

- Regularly check your growing environment to ensure optimal conditions. Keep a log of temperature, humidity, and any changes in the appearance of your mushrooms.
- Always wash your hands and tools before handling mushrooms or substrate. Keep the growing area clean and free from pests.
- Growing mushrooms can take time, so be patient and attentive. Each species has its own growth timeline, and maintaining the right conditions is key to success.

By carefully choosing and preparing your growing location, you'll create a thriving environment for your mushrooms. Whether indoors or outdoors, the right setup will help you enjoy the rewarding experience of homegrown mushrooms. Happy cultivating, and may your mushrooms flourish!

When to Grow Mushroom

Timing can be just as important as location and setup when it comes to mushroom cultivation. Understanding when to grow mushrooms can help ensure a successful and bountiful harvest. Let's break it down together.

Indoor Cultivation Timing

The beauty of growing mushrooms indoors is that you can cultivate them year-round, regardless of the season. Since you have control over the environment, you can create the ideal conditions for your mushrooms at any time. Here are some tips for indoor cultivation:

Year-Round Growing: With the right setup, including proper temperature, humidity, and lighting, you can grow mushrooms indoors all year long. This flexibility is perfect for those who want a steady supply of fresh mushrooms.

Climate Control: Use heaters, air conditioners, humidifiers, and grow lights to maintain the optimal environment for your mushrooms. Keeping conditions stable will allow you to grow your mushrooms whenever you want.

Consistent Monitoring: Regularly check and adjust your setup to ensure that your mushrooms have the best possible conditions. Indoor growing allows for fine-tuning, so take advantage of it!

Daily Care and Maintenance

1. **Check Daily**: Inspect your mushrooms daily for signs of growth and any issues like mold or pests.
2. **Maintain Humidity**: Keep the humidity high by misting and using a humidifier. Mushrooms need a moist environment to fruit properly.
3. **Adjust Lighting**: Ensure your mushrooms are receiving the right amount

of light. Adjust the position of your grow lights or containers if necessary.

4. **Ventilation**: Good airflow is essential. Use small fans to circulate air and prevent carbon dioxide buildup.

Solution to Common Issues

1. **Contamination**: If you notice mold or unwanted fungi, remove the affected area immediately. Clean the space thoroughly and ensure your substrate was properly sterilized.
2. **Drying Out**: If the substrate is too dry, increase misting and check your humidifier. You may need to add a humidity tent or dome over the growing area.
3. **Slow Growth**: If mushrooms are growing slowly, check temperature and light conditions. Ensure they're within the optimal range for your species.

Harvesting

Mushrooms are typically ready to harvest when the caps have fully opened but before they start to release spores. This varies by species, so familiarize yourself with the specific signs for your chosen mushrooms.

Harvesting Technique: Use a sharp knife to cut mushrooms at the base, leaving the substrate undisturbed. Clean the knife between cuts to prevent contamination.

Post-Harvest Care: After harvesting, continue to care for the remaining mushrooms. Some species will produce multiple flushes, so keep the environment stable and moist.

By carefully setting up and maintaining your indoor cultivation space, you'll create the perfect environment for growing healthy, bountiful mushrooms. Indoor growing offers the advantage of year-round cultivation, allowing you to enjoy fresh mushrooms whenever you like. So, gather your supplies, set up your space, and watch your mushroom garden flourish!

Outdoor Cultivation Timing

Outdoor mushroom cultivation is a rewarding endeavor that allows you to take advantage of natural conditions to grow delicious, fresh mushrooms. Let's explore the details of seasonal considerations and maintenance tips.

Seasonal Considerations

Spring

Ideal Conditions: Spring offers mild temperatures and increased rainfall, making it a great time to start your outdoor mushroom cultivation.

Preparation: Begin preparing your substrate and inoculating in late winter to early spring. This timing allows mushrooms to start growing as soon as conditions are right.

Summer

Warm-Weather Varieties: Certain oyster mushrooms and other warm-tolerant species can thrive in summer.

Shading and Watering: Ensure your setup is well-shaded and keep the substrate moist.

Frequent watering or misting may be necessary to maintain high humidity.

Protection: Consider using shade cloths or other covers to protect your mushrooms from the intense sun and heat.

Fall

Optimal Growing Season: Like spring, fall offers cool, moist conditions perfect for many mushroom species.

Early Start: Prepare and inoculate your substrate in late summer to take full advantage of the fall growing season.

Extended Harvest: Fall conditions often allow for extended harvesting periods before winter sets in.

Winter

Challenges: Cold temperatures and potential frost make winter cultivation challenging but not impossible.

Cold-Tolerant Species: Some oyster varieties and enoki mushrooms can tolerate cold conditions. Grow these in late fall through early spring.

Insulation: Use straw, mulch, or row covers to insulate your substrate from freezing. Growing in a greenhouse or cold frame can also help extend the season.

Daily Care and Maintenance

Monitoring Conditions

- *Humidity*: Outdoor mushrooms need a moist environment. Use a misting system or water manually to keep the substrate damp. Avoid water logging by ensuring good drainage.
- *Temperature*: Monitor temperatures and provide additional shading or insulation as needed to protect your mushrooms from extreme conditions.

Pest Control

- *Barriers*: Use physical barriers like netting or fences to keep out pests such as rodents, insects, and birds.

- *Natural Repellents*: Introduce natural predators or use organic repellents to manage pests without harming your mushrooms.

Regular Inspection

- *Health Checks*: Regularly inspect your mushrooms for signs of contamination, pests, or disease. Remove any affected mushrooms to prevent the spread of problems.
- *Maintenance*: Keep the growing area clean and free of debris. This helps minimize the risk of contamination and creates a healthy environment for your mushrooms.

Harvesting and Post-Harvest Care

When to Harvest

- *Timing*: Harvest mushrooms when the caps are fully opened but before they start to release spores. This timing ensures the best flavor and texture.

- *Technique*: Use a sharp knife to cut the mushrooms at the base. Be gentle to avoid disturbing the substrate or other growing mushrooms.

Post-Harvest Care

- *Storing*: Store fresh mushrooms in a cool, dry place. They can be kept in the refrigerator for up to a week.
- *Preservation*: For longer storage, consider drying, freezing, or pickling your mushrooms. Each method helps preserve the mushrooms' flavor and nutritional value.

By carefully selecting your outdoor growing location, preparing your substrate, and maintaining optimal conditions, you can enjoy a bountiful harvest of fresh mushrooms. Outdoor cultivation allows you to harness the natural environment to grow delicious and nutritious mushrooms right in your backyard.

Specific Mushroom Species Growing Season

Growing different mushroom species requires understanding their unique seasonal preferences and optimal growing conditions. Here's a detailed look at the growing seasons for specific mushroom species, along with tips to maximize your yields.

Button Mushrooms
Growing Season: Year-round (indoors), Spring and Fall (outdoors)

Indoor Cultivation: Button mushrooms can be grown indoors all year long. Maintain temperatures between 55-70°F (13-21°C) and ensure high humidity levels.
Outdoor Cultivation: In temperate climates, the best times to grow button mushrooms outdoors are during the cool, moist conditions of spring and fall. Prepare beds or containers with composted manure or rich organic matter.

Tips:

1. Start your outdoor cultivation in early spring after the last frost or in early fall before the first frost.
2. Provide shade to protect from direct sunlight and keep the soil consistently moist but not waterlogged.

Oyster Mushrooms (Pleurotus spp.)
Growing Season: Year-round (indoors), Spring and Fall (outdoors)

Indoor Cultivation: Oyster mushrooms are versatile and can thrive indoors throughout the year. Ideal temperatures range from 55-75°F (13-24°C) depending on the species.

Outdoor Cultivation: The best times to grow oyster mushrooms outdoors are during the mild temperatures and higher humidity of spring and fall. They can also be grown on logs, straw, or sawdust outdoors.

<u>Tips</u>:

1. For spring cultivation, start in late winter to early spring.
2. For fall cultivation, begin in late summer to early fall.
3. Regularly mist the substrate to maintain humidity and consider using a shade cloth during hot periods.

Shiitake Mushrooms (Lentinula edodes)
Growing Season: Spring, Fall (outdoors), Year-round (indoors on sawdust blocks)

Indoor Cultivation: Shiitake can be grown indoors year-round on sawdust blocks. Optimal temperatures are between 55-75°F (13-24°C).
Outdoor Cultivation: Best grown on hardwood logs (oak, maple) in spring and fall. Inoculate logs in late winter or early spring, or late summer for a fall start.

Tips:

Logs inoculated in spring can produce mushrooms in the same fall, while logs inoculated in fall will typically fruit the following spring. Keep logs in a shaded moist area and water them during dry periods to maintain moisture.

Lion's Mane Mushrooms (Hericium erinaceus)
Growing Season: Fall and Spring (outdoors), Year-round (indoors)

Indoor Cultivation: Grow lion's mane mushrooms indoors year-round with temperatures between 60-75°F (15-24°C).
Outdoor Cultivation: Ideal for fall and spring outdoors when temperatures are cooler. They can be grown on hardwood logs or sawdust.

<u>Tips</u>:

1. Inoculate logs in late winter or early spring for a spring start, or in late summer for fall cultivation.
2. Maintain high humidity and protect from direct sunlight.

Enoki Mushrooms (Flammulina velutipes)
Growing Season: Late Fall, Winter, and Early Spring (outdoors), Year-round (indoors)

Indoor Cultivation: Enoki mushrooms thrive indoors year-round in cool temperatures between 45-65°F (7-18°C).
Outdoor Cultivation: Best grown during the colder months of late fall, winter, and early spring when temperatures naturally drop.

Tips:

1. Outdoor cultivation can be tricky in very cold climates, so consider a greenhouse or cold frame to extend the growing season.
2. Provide a moist environment and protect from freezing temperatures.

Portobello and Cremini Mushrooms (Agaricus bisporus)

Growing Season: Year-round (indoors), Spring and Fall (outdoors)

Indoor Cultivation: These mushrooms can be cultivated indoors throughout the year with temperatures between 60-70°F (15-21°C) and high humidity.

Outdoor Cultivation: Grow outdoors in the cooler temperatures and higher humidity of spring and fall. Prepare rich composted beds for best results.

<u>Tips</u>:

1. For outdoor cultivation, start in early spring or early fall, ensuring the growing area remains shaded and moist.
2. Maintain steady moisture in the substrate to encourage consistent growth.

Reishi Mushrooms (Ganoderma lucidum)

Growing Season: Spring to Fall (outdoors), Year-round (indoors)

Indoor Cultivation: Reishi mushrooms can be grown year-round indoors using hardwood sawdust blocks. They prefer temperatures between 70-85°F (21-29°C).

Outdoor Cultivation: Best grown on hardwood logs outdoors from spring to fall. Inoculate logs in early spring for the best results.

Tips:

Logs inoculated in early spring will usually start fruiting by summer and can continue producing until fall. Keep logs in a shaded, humid area and water them during dry spells.

Understanding the optimal growing seasons for different mushroom species is crucial for successful cultivation. By aligning your growing practices with the natural preferences of each species, you can maximize your yields and enjoy fresh mushrooms throughout the year.

<u>Indoor Cultivation</u>: Provides the flexibility to grow mushrooms year-round with controlled conditions. Ideal for consistent production and experimenting with different species.

<u>Outdoor Cultivation</u>: Utilizes natural seasonal conditions to grow mushrooms in a more traditional setting. Ideal for large-scale cultivation and using natural substrates like logs. By tailoring your cultivation techniques to the specific needs of each mushroom species and their preferred growing seasons, you'll be well on your way to becoming a successful mushroom cultivator.

Final Tips for Successful Mushroom Cultivation

Consistent Monitoring and Maintenance

Daily Checks: Regularly inspect your mushrooms and their growing environment. Look for signs of contamination, pests, or other issues.

Environment Control: For indoor cultivation, use thermometers and hygrometers to monitor temperature and humidity levels. Adjust equipment as needed to maintain optimal conditions.

Watering and Misting: Keep the substrate consistently moist but not waterlogged. For outdoor setups, this might mean regular watering during dry spells, while indoor setups may require misting several times a day.

Hygiene and Sanitation

Cleanliness: Always wash your hands before handling mushrooms or substrate. Use clean tools and equipment to prevent contamination.

Sterilization: Ensure that your substrate is properly sterilized or pasteurized before inoculation to kill off any competing organisms.

Protect from Contaminants: Keep your growing area clean and free from debris. Use air filters for indoor setups to minimize airborne contaminants.

Proper Inoculation Techniques

Even Distribution: Ensure the mushroom spawn is evenly mixed into the substrate. Uneven distribution can lead to poor colonization and uneven fruiting.

Sealing: For indoor setups, seal containers or grow bags properly to maintain humidity and prevent contamination.

Optimizing Light and Airflow

Indirect Light: Most mushrooms prefer low light conditions. Indirect sunlight or low-intensity grow lights work best. Avoid direct sunlight, which can dry out the substrate.

Ventilation: Ensure good airflow around your growing area to prevent the buildup of carbon dioxide and promote healthy mushroom growth. Small fans can help improve ventilation for indoor setups.

Adjusting for Seasonal Changes

Temperature Management: Adjust your indoor climate control systems seasonally to maintain stable growing conditions. For outdoor setups, consider using shade cloths or row covers to protect from extreme weather.

Humidity Control: Use humidifiers, misting systems, or regular manual misting to maintain high humidity levels, especially during dry seasons or indoor heating periods.

Pests and Disease Management

Natural Barriers: Use physical barriers like netting or fencing to protect outdoor mushrooms from pests.

Organic Repellents: Introduce natural predators or use organic repellents to manage pests without harming your mushrooms.

Early Detection: Act quickly at the first sign of disease or pests. Remove affected mushrooms and substrate to prevent the spread of issues.

Harvesting and Post-Harvest Care

Timely Harvesting: Harvest mushrooms at the right time—when the caps are fully opened but before they release spores. This ensures the best flavor and texture.

Gentle Handling: Use a sharp knife to cut mushrooms at the base. Handle them gently to avoid bruising and contamination.

Storage: Store fresh mushrooms in a cool, dry place. They can be refrigerated for up to a week. For longer storage, consider drying, freezing, or pickling.

Maximizing Yields

Multiple Flushes: Many mushrooms produce several flushes of growth. Continue to care for the substrate after the first harvest to encourage additional flushes.

Substrate Reuse: Some substrates can be reused or composted to enrich new batches of substrate. This can be an efficient way to extend your growing materials.

Experiment and Record-Keeping

Experiment: Don't be afraid to try different methods, substrates, and species to find what works best for you. Each environment is unique, and experimentation can lead to better results.

Keep Records: Maintain a detailed log of your cultivation process, including dates, environmental conditions, and any issues encountered. This information can help you refine your techniques and improve future yields.

Community and Learning

Join a Community: Engage with other mushroom cultivators through online forums, local gardening clubs, or social media groups. Sharing experiences and tips can provide valuable insights and support.

Continuous Learning: Stay informed about new techniques, species, and innovations in mushroom cultivation. Read books, attend workshops, and watch tutorials to expand your knowledge.

Solutions to Common Issues
Contamination

Identify Early: Look for unusual colors, textures, or odors that indicate contamination. Remove contaminated sections promptly.

Prevent Spread: Clean your growing area thoroughly and maintain strict hygiene practices to prevent future contamination.

Poor Growth

Check Conditions: Reevaluate temperature, humidity, and light levels to ensure they meet the needs of your mushroom species.

Substrate Quality: Ensure your substrate is nutrient-rich and properly prepared. Consider supplementing with additional nutrients if growth is slow.

Low Yields

Improve Techniques: Fine-tune your inoculation, watering, and environmental control techniques. Small adjustments can lead to significant improvements in yields.

Use Quality Spawn: Invest in high-quality, fresh mushroom spawn from reputable suppliers. The quality of the spawn directly affects the success of your cultivation.

By following these tips and remaining attentive to the needs of your mushrooms, you'll create a thriving environment for them to grow.

CHAPTER 4

Mushroom Life Cycle

Understanding the life cycle of mushrooms is essential for successful cultivation. This fascinating process unfolds in several stages, each crucial to the growth and development of the mushrooms we eventually harvest. Let's explore the mushroom life cycle together, step-by-step.

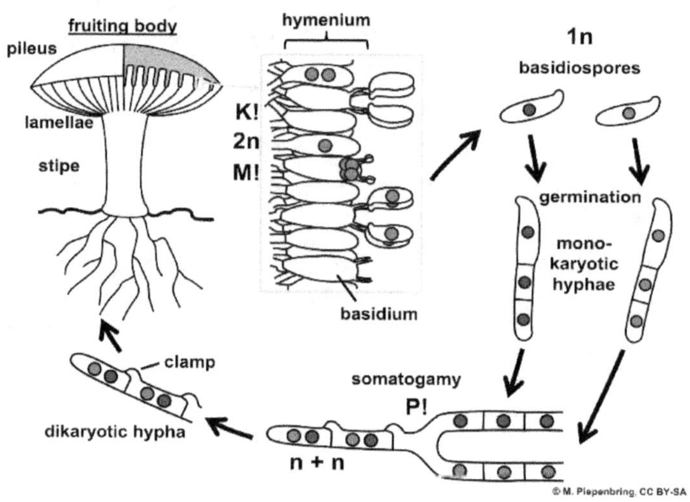

1. Spore Germination

It all starts with spores, the tiny reproductive units of mushrooms. Think of spores as the seeds of the fungal world. Each mushroom releases millions of spores into the environment, hoping that a few will land in suitable conditions to germinate.

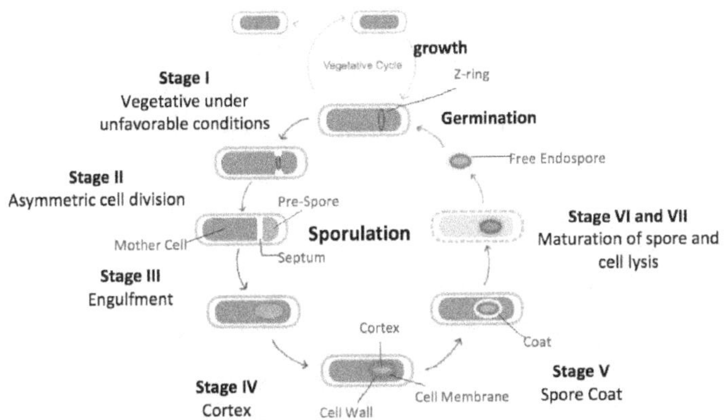

Conditions Needed:

Moisture: Spores need a moist environment to begin germinating.

Substrate: A nutritious substrate such as wood, compost, or soil provides the necessary nutrients for growth.

Temperature: The right temperature varies by species but generally falls within a specific range that supports germination.

Once spores find the right conditions, they begin to grow and form thread-like structures called hyphae.

2. Hyphal Growth and Mycelium Formation

As spores germinate, they develop into hyphae. Hyphae are tiny, thread-like filaments that spread out and explore the substrate for nutrients. When two compatible hyphae meet, they fuse together to form a network known as mycelium.

Mycelium:

Nutrient Absorption: Mycelium absorbs nutrients from the substrate, fueling its growth and development.

Colonization: The mycelium spreads throughout the substrate, creating a vast, interconnected network that can be considered the "body" of the fungus.

Think of mycelium as the roots of a plant, working underground to gather the necessary resources for future growth.

3. Mycelium Maturation

Once the mycelium has thoroughly colonized the substrate, it continues to mature. This stage can take anywhere from a few weeks to several months, depending on the mushroom species and growing conditions.

Key Factors:

Temperature: Consistent temperatures help mycelium thrive.

Humidity: High humidity levels support healthy growth.

Oxygen: Proper ventilation is essential to provide the mycelium with the oxygen it needs.

During this stage, the mycelium builds up the energy required to produce mushrooms.

4. Primordia Formation

When conditions are just right, the mature mycelium forms tiny knots called primordia, which are the first visible signs of mushroom development. These primordia will grow into full-sized mushrooms.

Triggers for Primordia Formation:

Temperature Change: A drop in temperature often signals the mycelium to start forming primordia.

Light: Exposure to light can also trigger mushroom formation, although some species grow in the dark.

Humidity: Maintaining high humidity levels is crucial during this stage.

Primordia formation is an exciting moment in mushroom cultivation, as it means that fruiting bodies are on their way.

5. Mushroom Development

The primordia develop into pinheads, which then expand into full-grown mushrooms. This stage is relatively fast, often taking just a few days.

<u>Growth Factors:</u>

Moisture: Ensure the substrate remains moist but not waterlogged.

Ventilation: Good airflow prevents the buildup of carbon dioxide, which can hinder mushroom growth.

Light: While not all mushrooms require light, some species benefit from low-intensity light exposure.

Watching your mushrooms grow from tiny pinheads to mature fruiting bodies is one of the most rewarding parts of the cultivation process.

6. Spore Release and Life Cycle Continuation

Once mushrooms reach maturity, they release spores into the environment to start the life cycle all over again. The gills, pores, or other spore-producing structures under the mushroom cap release spores, which are carried away by the wind or water.

Harvesting Tips:

Timing: Harvest mushrooms just before or as they begin to release spores for the best flavor and texture.

Technique: Use a sharp knife to cut the mushrooms at the base, being careful not to damage the mycelium, which can continue producing more mushrooms.

By understanding the mushroom life cycle, you can better appreciate the delicate balance of conditions needed for each stage of growth. Whether you're growing mushrooms indoors in controlled environments or outdoors in your garden, keeping these stages in mind will help you create the perfect conditions for your mushrooms to thrive.

Remember, patience and observation are key. Each stage of the life cycle offers its own challenges and rewards, and with time, you'll become more attuned to the needs of your fungi friends.

Environmental Factors Affecting Growth

Understanding the environmental factors that affect mushroom growth is crucial for successful cultivation. By controlling these factors, you can create the optimal conditions for your mushrooms to thrive. Let's explore these key factors in detail.

1. Temperature

Temperature plays a vital role in every stage of mushroom growth, from spore germination to fruiting. Different species have specific temperature ranges they prefer, so it's essential to know the requirements of the mushrooms you're cultivating.

Spore Germination: Most spores require temperatures between 70-80°F (21-27°C) to germinate effectively.

Mycelium Growth: Ideal temperatures for mycelial growth usually range from 60-75°F (15-24°C). However, some species like shiitake can thrive at slightly cooler temperatures.

Fruiting: Fruiting bodies often need a slight temperature drop to trigger formation. For example, oyster mushrooms prefer fruiting temperatures between 55-65°F (13-18°C), while button mushrooms prefer 55-70°F (13-21°C).

<u>Tips:</u>

1. Use heating mats or space heaters to maintain warm temperatures for germination and mycelium growth.
2. To initiate fruiting, reduce the temperature slightly to simulate the natural conditions that signal mushrooms to produce fruiting bodies.

2. Humidity

Mushrooms require high humidity levels to grow properly. Both mycelium and fruiting bodies thrive in moist environments.

Mycelium Growth: Maintain humidity levels around 85-90% to support healthy mycelium development.

Fruiting Bodies: Fruiting mushrooms need even higher humidity levels, typically between 90-95%.

Tips:

1. Use a hygrometer to monitor humidity levels in your growing area.
2. For indoor setups, use humidifiers or misting systems to maintain the desired humidity.
3. For outdoor cultivation, water regularly and consider using a shade cloth or plastic cover to retain moisture.

3. Light

While mushrooms don't photosynthesize, light can still influence their growth, particularly during the fruiting stage.

Mycelium Growth: Most mycelium prefers dark or dimly lit conditions.

Fruiting: Some species, like oyster and shiitake mushrooms, require light to fruit. Indirect sunlight or low-intensity fluorescent lights work well.

Tips:

1. For indoor cultivation, provide 12 hours of light and 12 hours of darkness to simulate natural light cycles.
2. Avoid direct sunlight, as it can dry out the substrate and harm the mycelium.

4. Airflow and CO2 Levels

Mushrooms need proper airflow to grow, as stagnant air can lead to the buildup of carbon dioxide (CO_2), which inhibits fruiting.

Mycelium Growth: While mycelium can tolerate higher CO2 levels, it still needs some fresh air exchange.

Fruiting Bodies: Fruiting mushrooms require fresh air to develop properly. High CO2 levels can lead to deformed mushrooms with elongated stems and small caps.

<u>Tips:</u>

1. Ensure good ventilation in your growing area by using fans or opening windows.
2. For indoor setups, consider installing an exhaust fan to remove excess CO2.
3. Be mindful of maintaining humidity while increasing airflow, as too much air movement can dry out the substrate.

5. Substrate Quality

The substrate provides the nutrients needed for mycelium growth and mushroom development. The type and quality of substrate can significantly impact yields and mushroom health.

Nutrient Content: Use substrates rich in organic matter. Common substrates include straw, sawdust, composted manure, and hardwood logs. *pH Levels*: Most mushrooms prefer slightly acidic to neutral pH levels (5.5 to 7.5).

Tips:

1. Choose a substrate that matches the needs of your specific mushroom species.
2. Supplement substrates with additional nutrients if necessary, such as adding bran to sawdust or gypsum to straw.
3. Regularly check and adjust the pH levels of your substrate.

6. Contamination Control

Contaminants like mold, bacteria, and pests can hinder mushroom growth and ruin your crop. Maintaining a clean growing environment is essential.

Hygiene: Always work with clean hands and tools. Sterilize or pasteurize your substrate before use.

Environment: Keep your growing area clean and free from debris. Use air filters to reduce airborne contaminants.

Tips:

1. Regularly inspect your growing area and mushrooms for signs of contamination.
2. Remove any contaminated substrate or mushrooms promptly to prevent the spread of disease.
3. Use protective gear, such as gloves and masks, when handling sterile substrates and spawn.

By carefully controlling these environmental factors, you can create the ideal conditions for your mushrooms to thrive. Each species may have specific preferences, so always research and tailor your approach to meet their unique needs.

CHAPTER 5

Cultivation Methods

When it comes to growing mushrooms, there are several cultivation methods you can choose from, each with its own set of advantages and considerations. You can decide which one suits your needs best after going through this chapter. Whether you're working with a small indoor setup or planning a larger outdoor garden, there's a method here for everyone.

1. Growing Mushrooms on Logs

Growing mushrooms on logs is a traditional and natural method that works particularly well for species like shiitake, oyster, and lion's mane mushrooms. This method mimics how mushrooms grow in the wild and can be done outdoors in a shaded area or even indoors if you have the space.

<u>Steps:</u>

1. *Select Logs*: Choose hardwood logs such as oak, maple, or beech. Freshly cut logs are ideal, as they contain the moisture and nutrients needed for mushroom growth.

2. *Inoculate Logs*: Drill holes into the logs and fill them with mushroom spawn. Seal the holes with wax to protect the spawn from contaminants.

3. *Incubation*: Place the logs in a shaded, humid area and water them regularly. The

mycelium will colonize the logs over several months.

4. *Fruiting*: Once the mycelium has fully colonized the logs, mushrooms will begin to fruit. This can take anywhere from six months to a year.

5.

Tips:

1. Keep logs off the ground to prevent contamination from soil organisms.
2. Maintain humidity by watering the logs or covering them with a tarp during dry periods.

2. Growing Mushrooms on Straw

Growing mushrooms on straw is a popular method for species like oyster mushrooms. Straw is readily available, easy to prepare, and provides an excellent growing medium.

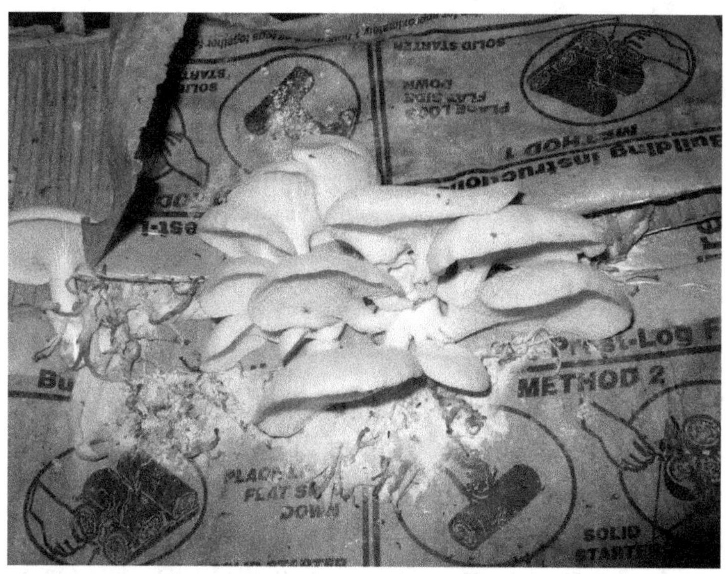

<u>Steps:</u>

1. *Prepare Straw*: Cut the straw into short pieces and pasteurize it by soaking it in hot water (160-170°F or 70-77°C) for an hour. This kills off any competing organisms.

2. *Inoculate Straw*: Drain the straw and mix it with mushroom spawn. Pack the mixture into plastic bags or containers with holes for airflow.

3. *Incubation*: Keep the bags or containers in a warm, dark place with high humidity. The mycelium will colonize the straw in a few weeks.
4. *Fruiting:* Once the substrate is fully colonized, move it to a location with indirect light and higher humidity to trigger fruiting.

Tips:

1. Use a fan to ensure proper air circulation and prevent CO2 buildup.
2. Mist the substrate regularly to maintain moisture levels.

3. Growing Mushrooms on Sawdust Blocks

This method is highly effective for a variety of mushrooms, including shiitake, lion's mane, and reishi. Sawdust blocks provide a nutrient-rich environment and can be used both indoors and outdoors.

<u>Steps:</u>

1. *Prepare Sawdust*: Use hardwood sawdust and supplement it with bran or other nutrients. Sterilize the sawdust by steaming it at high temperatures.
2. *Inoculate Sawdust*: Once cooled, mix the sawdust with mushroom spawn and pack it into sterilized plastic bags or containers.
3. *Incubation:* Place the bags or containers in a warm, dark place. The mycelium will colonize the sawdust within a few weeks to months.

4. *Fruiting*: After full colonization, cut slits in the bags to allow mushrooms to fruit. Move them to a humid, well-ventilated area with indirect light.

Tips:

1. Keep the environment clean to prevent contamination.
2. Monitor humidity and temperature closely, as sawdust blocks can dry out quickly.

4. Growing Mushrooms in a Grow Kit

If you're just starting out or looking for a simple way to grow mushrooms, a grow kit is an excellent choice. Kits come with everything you need, including a pre-colonized substrate.

<u>Steps:</u>

1. *Set Up Kit*: Follow the instructions provided with the kit. Typically, this involves opening the bag or box and placing it in a suitable environment.
2. *Maintain Conditions*: Keep the kit in a location with the right temperature and humidity. Mist the kit regularly to maintain moisture.
3. *Harvest*: Mushrooms will begin to fruit within a few days to weeks. Harvest them as they mature.

Tips:

1. Follow the kit instructions carefully for the best results.
2. Experiment with different types of kits to learn more about various mushroom species.

5. Growing Mushrooms in Outdoor Beds

Creating outdoor mushroom beds is a great method for species like wine cap (Stropharia), garden giant, and even some oyster mushrooms.

This method involves using mulch, straw, or wood chips in a garden setting.

<u>Steps:</u>

1. *Prepare Bed*: Choose a shaded, well-drained area. Lay down a layer of cardboard to suppress weeds and then add layers of straw, wood chips, or other organic material.
2. Inoculate Bed: Spread mushroom spawn evenly across the substrate layers.
3. *Maintain Bed*: Water the bed regularly to keep it moist. The mycelium will colonize the substrate over several months.
4. *Fruiting*: Mushrooms will start to fruit when conditions are right, typically in the spring and fall.

Tips:

1. Add more organic material to the bed periodically to feed the mycelium.
2. Protect the bed from heavy rain or extreme weather conditions.

Each cultivation method has its own set of benefits and challenges. Your choice will depend on factors like the mushroom species you want to grow, available space, and your level of experience.

Logs are great for long-term outdoor cultivation. Straw is ideal for fast-growing species like oyster mushrooms. Sawdust blocks provide a rich growing medium for various indoor and outdoor mushrooms. Grow kits are perfect for beginners or those with limited space. Outdoor beds offer a natural, low-maintenance way to grow mushrooms in your garden. Experiment with different methods to find what works best for you.

However, before getting started you need to know about substrate and different Inoculation Techniques

Substrate Selection and Preparation

Selecting and preparing the right substrate is crucial for successful mushroom cultivation. The substrate provides the essential nutrients that mushrooms need to grow. Let's explore the various substrates you can use and how to prepare them effectively.

Understanding Substrates

A substrate is any material that supports the growth of mushroom mycelium. Different mushrooms prefer different substrates, so it's important to choose one that matches the needs of the species you're cultivating. Common substrates include straw, wood chips, sawdust, compost, and even coffee grounds.

Common Substrates for Mushroom Cultivation

Straw

- Ideal for: Oyster mushrooms, wine cap mushrooms.
- Why it's good: Straw is easy to find, inexpensive, and provides a good structure for mycelium to colonize.

Hardwood Sawdust

- Ideal for: Shiitake, lion's mane, reishi mushrooms.

- Why it's good: Hardwood sawdust is nutrient-rich and closely mimics the natural growing conditions for many mushrooms.

Wood Chips

- Ideal for: Wine cap, garden giant, and some oyster mushrooms.
- Why it's good: Wood chips break down slowly, providing a long-lasting nutrient source for mushrooms.

Composted Manure
- Ideal for: Button mushrooms, portobello mushrooms.
- Why it's good: Composted manure is rich in nutrients and provides an excellent growing medium for many gourmet mushrooms.

Coffee Grounds
- Ideal for: Oyster mushrooms.

- Why it's good: Coffee grounds are high in nitrogen and can be a good supplemental substrate when mixed with other materials.

How to Prepare Substrates

Preparation is key to ensuring that your substrate is free of contaminants and ready to support mushroom growth. Here's how to prepare the most common substrates:

Straw Preparation

- *Cutting*: Cut the straw into short pieces (about 1-2 inches). This increases the surface area for mycelium colonization.
- *Pasteurization:* Pasteurize the straw by soaking it in hot water (160-170°F or 70-77°C) for about an hour. This kills off competing organisms while preserving beneficial microbes.
- *Draining:* After pasteurization, drain the straw thoroughly to remove excess water.

Hardwood Sawdust Preparation

- *Mixing*: Mix the hardwood sawdust with a nutrient supplement like bran (10-20% by volume) to enhance growth.
- *Sterilization*: Sterilize the sawdust mixture by steaming it at 250°F (121°C) for 90 minutes. This ensures that all potential contaminants are eliminated.
- *Cooling*: Allow the sawdust to cool completely in a clean environment before inoculating with mushroom spawn.

Wood Chips Preparation

- *Hydration*: Soak the wood chips in water for 24 hours to hydrate them fully.
- *Pasteurization*: Similar to straw, pasteurize the wood chips by soaking them in hot water (160-170°F or 70-77°C) for an hour.
- *Draining:* Drain the wood chips thoroughly before use.

Composted Manure Preparation

- *Aging*: Ensure the manure is well-composted and aged to avoid high ammonia levels, which can inhibit mycelium growth.
- *Mixing:* Mix the composted manure with straw or other organic material to improve texture and aeration.
- *Pasteurization*: Pasteurize the mixture by heating it to 160-170°F (70-77°C) for an hour to kill any pathogens.

Coffee Grounds Preparation

- *Collection*: Collect fresh, used coffee grounds.
- *Pasteurization*: While coffee grounds are already pasteurized during the brewing process, it's still a good idea to mix them with other substrates and pasteurize the mixture again.
- *Mixing*: Combine the coffee grounds with straw or sawdust to create a balanced substrate.

Inoculating the Substrate

Once your substrate is prepared, the next step is to inoculate it with mushroom spawn.

Here's how to do it:

1. *Cleanliness*: Work in a clean environment to minimize the risk of contamination. Use gloves and sanitize your tools.
2. *Mixing:* Thoroughly mix the mushroom spawn into the prepared substrate. Ensure

even distribution to promote uniform colonization.

3. *Packing:* Pack the inoculated substrate into containers or grow bags, leaving some space for airflow.

4. *Incubation*: Place the containers or bags in a warm, dark place to allow the mycelium to colonize the substrate fully. This can take a few weeks to a few months, depending on the species and conditions.

Choosing and preparing the right substrate is a critical step in mushroom cultivation. By understanding the needs of your mushroom species and following these preparation guidelines, you can create an ideal environment for your mushrooms to grow

Monitoring and Maintenance

During the incubation period, it's important to monitor and maintain the conditions to ensure successful colonization

Inoculation Techniques

Inoculating your substrate with mushroom spawn is a crucial step in the cultivation process. This is where you introduce the mushroom spores or mycelium to the prepared substrate, setting the stage for growth and development. There are several techniques you can use, each suited to different types of substrates and growing conditions. Let's explore these methods together.

Why Inoculation is Important

Inoculation is the process of adding mushroom spawn to your substrate. This step is vital because it kickstarts the colonization process, where the mycelium spreads throughout the substrate, ultimately leading to the growth of mushrooms. Proper inoculation ensures that the mycelium has a good start and reduces the risk of contamination.

Common Inoculation Techniques

Spore Inoculation

Spore inoculation involves introducing spores directly to the substrate. This method is often used in laboratory settings or for growing mushrooms from scratch.

<u>Steps:</u>

1. *Prepare Spore Syringe*: Spores are typically suspended in a sterile solution inside a syringe.
2. *Inject Spores*: Inject the spore solution into the prepared substrate. This is often done in multiple spots to ensure even distribution.
3. *Seal and Incubate*: Seal the inoculated substrate and place it in a warm, dark area to allow the spores to germinate and develop into mycelium.

<u>Tips:</u>

1. Maintain sterile conditions to prevent contamination.
2. Be patient, as spore germination can take a few weeks.

Grain Spawn Inoculation

Grain spawn is a popular and effective method for inoculating a wide range of substrates. The grain, such as rye or millet, is colonized with mycelium and then used to inoculate the main substrate.

<u>Steps:</u>

1. *Break Up Grain Spawn*: Gently break up the grain spawn to separate the kernels without damaging the mycelium.
2. *Mix with Substrate*: Mix the grain spawn evenly into the prepared substrate. Ensure thorough mixing for uniform colonization.

3. *Pack and Incubate*: Pack the inoculated substrate into containers or bags, and place them in a warm, dark area for incubation.

Tips:

1. Use a high spawn rate (10-20% of the substrate volume) for faster colonization.
2. Keep the incubation area clean and well-ventilated.

Plug Spawn Inoculation

Plug spawn is commonly used for inoculating logs and outdoor cultivation. It consists of wooden dowels colonized with mushroom mycelium.

Steps:

1. *Drill Holes in Logs*: Drill holes in the logs at regular intervals, about 1-2 inches deep and spaced a few inches apart.

2. *Insert Plug Spawn*: Insert the plug spawn into the drilled holes and tap them in securely with a mallet.
3. *Seal with Wax*: Seal the holes with melted wax to protect the spawn and prevent contamination.
4. *Place Logs for Incubation*: Place the inoculated logs in a shaded, humid area to allow the mycelium to colonize the wood.

<u>Tips:</u>

1. Use hardwood logs for better results.
2. Water the logs regularly to maintain moisture levels.

Liquid Culture Inoculation

Liquid culture involves suspending mycelium in a nutrient-rich liquid solution. This method allows for rapid colonization and is often used for commercial and large-scale mushroom cultivation.

Steps:

1. Prepare Liquid Culture: Use a sterile syringe to draw the liquid culture containing mycelium.
2. Inject into Substrate: Inject the liquid culture into multiple points of the substrate.
3. Seal and Incubate: Seal the inoculated substrate and incubate it in a warm, dark place.

Tips:

1. Maintain sterile conditions to avoid contamination.
2. Monitor the substrate regularly for signs of colonization.

Sawdust Spawn Inoculation

Sawdust spawn is another versatile and effective method, suitable for a variety of substrates including sawdust, wood chips, and even straw.

Steps:

1. Break Up Sawdust Spawn: Break up the sawdust spawn to ensure it can be evenly mixed with the substrate.
2. Mix with Substrate: Thoroughly mix the sawdust spawn into the prepared substrate.
3. Pack and Incubate: Pack the inoculated substrate into containers or bags and place them in a suitable incubation environment.

Tips:

1. Use a high spawn rate to ensure rapid colonization.
2. Ensure the substrate is adequately hydrated before inoculation.

General Tips for Successful Inoculation

Sterilization: Always work in a clean environment to minimize the risk of contamination. Sterilize your tools, hands, and workspace before starting.

Hydration: Ensure your substrate is properly hydrated. Too much or too little moisture can hinder mycelium growth.

Temperature: Maintain the optimal temperature for the species you are cultivating during the incubation period.

Patience and Observation: Monitor the substrate regularly for signs of contamination or mycelium growth. Be patient, as colonization can take time.

Inoculating your substrate is a crucial step in mushroom cultivation, and doing it correctly can set you up for a successful harvest.

Here's a quick recap of the methods:

Spore Inoculation: Best for lab settings and starting from scratch.

Grain Spawn: Ideal for rapid and uniform colonization of various substrates.

Plug Spawn: Perfect for outdoor log cultivation.

Liquid Culture: Suitable for rapid colonization and commercial use.

Sawdust Spawn: Versatile and effective for many types of substrates.

Choose the method that best fits your needs and resources, and enjoy the process of watching your mycelium grow and thrive

CHAPTER 6

Growing Different Mushroom Varieties

Growing mushrooms can be a deeply rewarding experience, especially when you tailor your cultivation techniques to suit the specific needs of different mushroom varieties. Each type of mushroom has its own unique requirements and quirks.

Cultivation Techniques for Common Edible Mushrooms

Button Mushrooms (Agaricus bisporus)

Button mushrooms are one of the most common and widely consumed mushrooms worldwide. They are known for their mild flavor and versatility in cooking.

Substrate: Composted manure or a mix of compost and straw.

Temperature: 65-75°F (18-24°C) for spawning, 55-65°F (13-18°C) for fruiting.

Humidity: High, around 85-95%.

Steps:

1. *Prepare Substrate*: Use well-composted manure mixed with straw. Pasteurize the mixture to kill any unwanted organisms.
2. *Inoculate*: Spread the button mushroom spawn evenly across the prepared substrate.
3. *Cover with Casing*: Once the mycelium has colonized the substrate (about 2-3 weeks), cover it with a casing layer made of peat moss and limestone.
4. *Fruiting*: Maintain a lower temperature and high humidity to initiate fruiting. Mushrooms will start to appear in 7-14 days.

<u>Tips:</u>

1. Regularly mist the casing layer to keep it moist.
2. Harvest when the caps are fully developed but still closed.

Shiitake Mushrooms (Lentinula edodes)

Shiitake mushrooms are prized for their rich, savory flavor and numerous health benefits. They are typically grown on hardwood logs or sawdust blocks.

Substrate: Hardwood logs (oak, beech, maple) or hardwood sawdust.

Temperature: 70-80°F (21-27°C) for incubation, 55-70°F (13-21°C) for fruiting.

Humidity: Moderate to high, around 75-85%.

Steps:

1. **Prepare Logs or Sawdust**: For logs, cut fresh hardwood logs and let them sit for a few weeks. For sawdust, mix with supplements and sterilize.
2. **Inoculate**: Drill holes into the logs and insert shiitake plug spawn. For sawdust, mix with shiitake spawn.
3. **Incubate**: Place logs in a shaded, humid area. For sawdust blocks, keep in a warm, dark place. Incubation can take 6-12 months for logs and a few weeks for sawdust.
4. **Fruiting**: Once fully colonized, soak logs in cold water for 24 hours to stimulate fruiting. Move sawdust blocks to a fruiting chamber with higher humidity and indirect light.

Tips:

1. Soak logs periodically to maintain moisture.
2. Harvest shiitake mushrooms when the caps are fully open but not yet flat.

Oyster Mushrooms (Pleurotus spp.)

Oyster mushrooms are known for their delicate texture and mild flavor. They are one of the easiest mushrooms to grow and can thrive on various substrates.

Substrate: Straw, coffee grounds, sawdust, or cardboard.

Temperature: 75-85°F (24-29°C) for incubation, 50-70°F (10-21°C) for fruiting.

Humidity: High, around 85-95%.

<u>Steps:</u>

1. **Prepare Substrate**: Cut and pasteurize the straw or other substrate material. For

coffee grounds, mix with another substrate like straw or cardboard.

2. **Inoculate**: Mix the substrate with oyster mushroom spawn and pack it into bags or containers with holes.

3. **Incubate**: Keep the bags in a warm, dark place for mycelium colonization, which takes about 2-3 weeks.

4. **Fruiting**: Move the bags to a cooler, humid area with indirect light. Mushrooms will start to fruit within a few days to weeks.

Tips:

1. Ensure good air circulation to prevent CO_2 buildup.

2. Harvest oyster mushrooms when the edges of the caps start to flatten out.

Lion's Mane Mushrooms (Hericium erinaceus)

Lion's Mane mushrooms are not only unique in appearance but also celebrated for their potential cognitive benefits and seafood-like flavor.

Substrate: Hardwood sawdust, supplemented with bran.

Temperature: 65-75°F (18-24°C) for incubation, 55-65°F (13-18°C) for fruiting.

Humidity: High, around 85-95%.

<u>Steps:</u>

1. *Prepare Substrate*: Mix hardwood sawdust with bran, then sterilize.
2. *Inoculate*: Mix the substrate with Lion's Mane spawn and pack into bags or containers.
3. *Incubate*: Place the bags in a warm, dark place for colonization, which takes about 2-3 weeks.
4. *Fruiting*: Once colonized, cut holes in the bags and move to a fruiting chamber with high humidity and indirect light.

Tips:

1. Mist the fruiting area regularly to maintain humidity.
2. Harvest when the spines are well-developed but still firm.

Enoki Mushrooms (Flammulina velutipes)

Enoki mushrooms are known for their long, thin stems and small caps. They have a mild, slightly fruity flavor and are often used in soups and salads.

Substrate: Hardwood sawdust, supplemented with bran.

Temperature: 70-75°F (21-24°C) for incubation, 45-60°F (7-15°C) for fruiting.

Humidity: Moderate to high, around 70-85%.

Steps:

1. *Prepare Substrate:* Mix hardwood sawdust with bran, then sterilize.
2. *Inoculate:* Mix the substrate with Enoki spawn and pack into narrow containers or bottles.
3. *Incubate:* Keep the containers in a warm, dark place for colonization, which takes about 2-3 weeks.
4. *Fruiting:* Move the containers to a cooler, dark place to initiate fruiting. Enoki mushrooms grow long and thin in low light.

Tips:

1. Keep the growing environment cool to encourage the characteristic long stems.
2. Harvest when the mushrooms are long and before the caps start to open wide.

Growing different mushroom varieties requires understanding their unique needs and adapting your techniques accordingly.

Specialty Mushrooms and Their Cultivation Requirements

Growing these mushrooms can be an exciting adventure, adding unique flavors, textures, and health benefits to your kitchen and beyond. These mushrooms often require specific conditions to grow, but with a little care and attention, you can successfully cultivate these exotic varieties at home. Let's dive into some of the most intriguing specialty mushrooms and their cultivation requirements.

Reishi Mushrooms (Ganoderma lucidum)

Reishi mushrooms, known as the "mushroom of immortality," are celebrated for their medicinal properties, including immune system support and anti-inflammatory effects.

Substrate: Hardwood logs (oak, maple) or hardwood sawdust.

Container: Logs for outdoor cultivation, bags or jars for indoor cultivation.

Environment: Warm and humid spaces.

Maitake Mushrooms (Grifola frondosa)

Maitake, also known as "Hen of the Woods," is a prized culinary and medicinal mushroom known for its rich, earthy flavor and health benefits.

Substrate: Hardwood logs (oak, maple) or hardwood sawdust.

Container: Logs for outdoor cultivation, bags or blocks for indoor cultivation.

Environment: Cool and shaded areas.

Black Trumpet Mushrooms (Craterellus cornucopioides)

Black Trumpet mushrooms are highly sought after for their smoky, rich flavor. They are somewhat challenging to cultivate but well worth the effort.

Substrate: Deciduous leaf litter and humus-rich soil.

Container: Outdoor garden beds.

Environment: Shaded and moist forest-like conditions.

Cordyceps Mushrooms (Cordyceps militaris)

Cordyceps are renowned for their medicinal properties, particularly for energy and stamina enhancement. They are primarily grown for their health benefits rather than culinary use.

Substrate: Grain, insect larvae, or synthetic nutrient media.

Container: Jars or plastic containers.

Environment: Warm and humid indoor settings.

Turkey Tail Mushrooms (Trametes versicolor)

Turkey Tail mushrooms are known for their striking colors and medicinal properties, particularly in boosting the immune system.

Substrate: Hardwood logs (oak, beech) or hardwood sawdust.

Container: Logs for outdoor cultivation, bags for indoor cultivation.

Environment: Shaded and humid areas.

CHAPTER 7

Common Issues in Mushroom Cultivation

Mushroom cultivation can be a wonderfully rewarding hobby, but like any growing endeavor, it comes with its share of challenges. Don't let these potential pitfalls discourage you. With a bit of knowledge and careful attention, most issues can be easily managed. Let's go through some of the most common problems you might encounter and how to address them.

Identifying and Addressing Contamination

One of the most frequent issues in mushroom cultivation is contamination by unwanted molds, bacteria, or other fungi. Contamination can spoil your substrate and ruin your crop.

Causes:

- Inadequate sterilization or pasteurization of the substrate.
- Poor hygiene practices.
- Contaminated spawn.

Solutions:

1. **Sterilize Properly**: Ensure your substrate is properly sterilized or pasteurized. This might involve boiling, steaming, or using a pressure cooker.
2. **Maintain Cleanliness**: Always wash your hands and use clean tools when handling your substrate and spawn. Working in a clean environment is crucial.
3. **Use Quality Spawn**: Purchase spawn from reputable suppliers to minimize the risk of contamination.

Poor Airflow

Mushrooms need fresh air to grow properly. Poor airflow can lead to CO2 buildup, which can stunt growth and cause deformities.

Causes:

- Overcrowded growing area.
- Insufficient ventilation.

Solutions:

1. **Improve Ventilation**: Ensure your growing area has good airflow. Use fans if necessary to circulate air.
2. **Space Out**: Don't overcrowd your containers or growing bags. Allow space for air to move around the mushrooms.

Inconsistent Humidity

Mushrooms thrive in high humidity, but the level needs to be consistent. Too little humidity can dry them out, while too much can promote mold growth.

Causes:

- Fluctuating environmental conditions.
- Improper misting practices.

Solutions:

1. **Use a Humidifier**: In a controlled indoor environment, a humidifier can help maintain consistent humidity levels.
2. **Mist Regularly**: If you're growing mushrooms in an outdoor or less controlled space, mist your growing area regularly but avoid over-watering.

Temperature Issues

Different mushroom species have specific temperature requirements. Incorrect temperatures can hinder growth or prevent fruiting altogether.

Causes:

- Growing the wrong mushroom species for your climate.
- Inadequate temperature control in indoor setups.

Solutions:

1. **Research Requirements**: Know the optimal temperature range for the mushroom species you are cultivating.
2. **Control Environment**: Use heaters, coolers, or grow tents to maintain the right temperature. For outdoor cultivation, choose species that are well-suited to your local climate.

Slow or No Growth

Sometimes mushrooms seem to take forever to grow, or they don't grow at all.

Causes:

- Inadequate substrate preparation.
- Incorrect environmental conditions.
- Contaminated or old spawn.

<u>Solutions:</u>

1. **Check Substrate**: Make sure your substrate is properly prepared and suitable for the mushroom species.
2. **Optimize Conditions**: Double-check temperature, humidity, and airflow. Adjust as needed.
3. **Use Fresh Spawn**: Ensure you're using fresh and high-quality spawn. Old or contaminated spawn can hinder growth.

Pests

Insects and other pests can be a problem, particularly in outdoor setups.

Causes:

- Open growing areas.
- Unclean environments.

<u>Solutions:</u>

1. **Cover and Protect**: Use mesh or nets to cover your growing area and keep pests out.
2. **Maintain Cleanliness**: Keep the area clean and free from debris that might attract pests.

Abnormal Fruiting Bodies

Mushrooms might sometimes grow in odd shapes or exhibit unusual colors.

Causes:

- Stress from environmental factors.
- Contamination or disease.

Solutions:

Monitor Conditions: Ensure your mushrooms are growing in optimal conditions without stress. **Check for Contamination**: Regularly inspect your mushrooms and substrate for signs of contamination and address any issues immediately.

Mushroom cultivation can be a bit tricky at times, but understanding the common issues and their solutions will go a long way in ensuring a successful harvest. By paying close attention to these factors and making adjustments as needed, you'll be well on your way to becoming a successful mushroom cultivator.

CHAPTER 8

Harvesting and Storage

Knowing When to Harvest

Harvesting mushrooms at the right time is crucial to enjoying their best flavor, texture, and nutritional value. Picking them too early or too late can affect the quality and yield of your crop. Let's explore how to determine the perfect time to harvest your mushrooms, ensuring you get the most out of your cultivation efforts.

Understanding the Growth Stages

Mushrooms go through several stages of growth, from tiny pins to mature fruiting bodies. Each stage has distinct characteristics:

Pin Stage: Small, pinhead-sized mushrooms start to appear.

Young Stage: Mushrooms begin to grow larger but still have closed caps.

Mature Stage: The caps start to open and flatten out.

Overripe Stage: The caps become overly flat or even upturned, and the texture may become tougher.

General Harvesting Guidelines

While each mushroom species has specific indicators, here are some general guidelines to help you determine when to harvest:

1. **Look at the Cap**: For many mushrooms, the best time to harvest is when the cap is still partially closed. This ensures the mushroom is tender and flavorful.
2. **Check the Veil**: For species like button mushrooms and portobellos, the partial veil (a thin membrane connecting the cap to the stem) starts to break as they mature. Harvest just before or as this veil breaks for optimal quality.
3. **Monitor Size**: Harvest mushrooms when they reach their full size but before they start to over-mature. Overgrown mushrooms can be less tasty and more prone to contamination.

Harvesting Specific Mushroom Varieties

Different mushrooms have unique signs indicating they're ready to be picked. Let's look at a few common varieties:

Button Mushrooms (Agaricus bisporus)

Timing: Harvest when the caps are still closed or just beginning to open. The veil should be intact or just starting to break.

Signs: The mushrooms should be firm and white (or brown, depending on the variety). Over-mature button mushrooms may turn a darker color and develop spots.

Shiitake Mushrooms (Lentinula edodes)

Timing: Pick when the caps are fully opened but still have a curled edge.

Signs: The cap should be between 2 to 4 inches in diameter and have a firm texture. If the edges start to flatten out, they may be overripe.

Oyster Mushrooms (Pleurotus spp.)

Timing: Harvest when the caps are still slightly curved and before they fully flatten.

Signs: The mushrooms should have a smooth, fresh appearance with no discoloration. They should be firm and slightly springy to the touch. Lion's Mane Mushrooms (Hericium erinaceus)

Timing: Pick when the spines are about 0.5 to 1 inch long.

Signs: The mushroom should be white and firm. Avoid harvesting when the spines begin to yellow or brown, indicating they are past their prime.

Enoki Mushrooms (Flammulina velutipes)

Timing: Harvest when the stems are long and the caps are small.

Signs: The mushrooms should be a creamy white color and have a delicate, crisp texture. They should be picked before the caps start to widen significantly.

How to Harvest

Proper harvesting techniques ensure you don't damage the mycelium, allowing for future flushes (batches) of mushrooms:

1. Clean Hands and Tools: Always wash your hands and sterilize any tools before harvesting to avoid contamination.
2. Twist and Pull: For most mushrooms, gently grasp the base and twist while pulling to remove the mushroom from the substrate.
3. Cutting: Use a sharp knife or scissors to cut the mushroom at the base if twisting seems likely to damage the substrate.
4. Leave the Mycelium Intact: Be careful not to disturb the underlying mycelium, as it's essential for future growth.

Post-Harvest Handling

Once harvested, handle your mushrooms with care to preserve their quality:

Clean Gently: Use a soft brush or cloth to remove any substrate or dirt. Avoid washing them, as mushrooms can absorb water and become soggy.

Store Properly: Place mushrooms in a paper bag or a breathable container and store them in the refrigerator. Avoid plastic bags, which can trap moisture and lead to spoilage.

Use Quickly: Fresh mushrooms are best used within a few days of harvesting for optimal flavor and texture.

Knowing when to harvest your mushrooms is a vital skill in cultivation.

Proper Harvesting Techniques

Harvesting your mushrooms is an exciting and rewarding part of the cultivation process. To ensure you get the best quality mushrooms and don't harm the mycelium, it's essential to use proper harvesting techniques. In this section, I'll guide you through the best practices for harvesting your fungi friends, so you can enjoy a bountiful and delicious yield.

Why Proper Harvesting Matters

Using the correct harvesting techniques is crucial for several reasons:

- **Preserves Quality**: Proper handling ensures your mushrooms are in their best condition for eating or selling.
- **Protects Mycelium**: Careful harvesting helps keep the mycelium intact, allowing for multiple flushes.
- **Prevents Contamination**: Clean harvesting practices reduce the risk of introducing contaminants to your grow area.

Tools You'll Need

While you can often harvest mushrooms with just your hands, having a few tools on hand can make the process easier and more efficient:

1. **Sharp Knife or Scissors**: For precise cutting without disturbing the substrate.

2. **Clean Gloves**: To prevent contamination from your hands.
3. **Soft Brush**: For gently cleaning any dirt or substrate off the mushrooms.

General Harvesting Steps

1. **Prepare Your Tools**: Ensure your knife or scissors are sharp and sterilized. Wear clean gloves to minimize contamination.
2. **Inspect the Mushrooms**: Check your mushrooms to ensure they are ready to harvest based on their growth stage, cap appearance, and size.
3. **Choose Your Method**: Decide whether you'll be twisting and pulling or cutting the mushrooms.

Harvesting Techniques

Let's look at the two primary methods for harvesting mushrooms:

1. Twist and Pull Method

This is a simple and commonly used method:

1. **Grip the Base**: Gently grasp the mushroom at the base, as close to the substrate as possible.
2. **Twist Gently**: Twist the mushroom while pulling upwards slightly. The twisting motion helps to release the mushroom from the substrate.
3. **Pull Up**: Continue twisting and gently pull the mushroom free from the substrate.

2. Cutting Method

This method is useful for delicate mushrooms or dense substrate:

1. Grip the Base: Hold the mushroom at the base to steady it.
2. Cut Cleanly: Use a sharp knife or scissors to cut the stem just above the substrate.

Make sure the cut is clean to prevent any tearing or damage to the mycelium.

After Harvesting

Once you've harvested your mushrooms, it's important to handle them properly to maintain their quality:

- **Clean Gently**: Use a soft brush to remove any substrate or dirt. Avoid washing the mushrooms as they can absorb water and become soggy.
- **Store Properly**: Place mushrooms in a paper bag or a breathable container. Store them in the refrigerator to keep them fresh. Avoid plastic bags, which can trap moisture and lead to spoilage.
- **Plan to Use Quickly:** Fresh mushrooms are best used within a few days of harvesting. Their flavor and texture are at their peak right after being picked.

Encouraging Future Flushes

After harvesting, it's essential to care for your substrate to encourage future flushes:

- **Rehydrate**: Mist the substrate lightly to maintain moisture levels.
- **Maintain Conditions**: Keep the growing environment consistent with the temperature, humidity, and airflow requirements of your mushrooms.
- **Inspect Regularly**: Check the substrate for any signs of contamination or pests, and address any issues promptly.

Proper harvesting techniques ensure you get the best quality mushrooms while preserving the health of your mycelium for future growth.

Storing Mushrooms for Freshness

Now that you've got a batch of fresh, homegrown mushrooms, it's crucial to store them properly to maintain their freshness, flavor, and texture. In this section, I'll guide you through the best practices for storing your mushrooms so you can enjoy them at their peak.

Immediate Post-Harvest Handling

Right after harvesting your mushrooms, it's essential to handle them with care:

Short-Term Storage

If you plan to use your mushrooms within a few days, here are some tips to keep them fresh:

Use Paper Bags or Breathable Containers

Why: Plastic bags trap moisture, which can make mushrooms slimy and lead to quicker spoilage. Paper bags or breathable containers allow for proper air circulation.

How: Place the mushrooms in a paper bag, fold the top loosely, and store them in the main compartment of your refrigerator. Avoid the crisper drawer, which can be too humid.

Keep Cool and Dry

- **Temperature**: Store your mushrooms at a cool temperature, ideally around 32-36°F (0-2°C).
- **Humidity**: Maintain a moderate humidity level. Too much humidity can cause mushrooms to rot, while too little can dry them out.

Longer-Term Storage

If you have a large harvest or want to extend the shelf life of your mushrooms, consider these methods:

Freezing

Freezing is a great way to preserve mushrooms for later use, especially if you plan to cook them:

- **Clean and Slice**: Clean the mushrooms and slice them if desired.
- **Blanching**: Blanch the mushrooms in boiling water for 1-2 minutes to preserve their texture and flavor. Quickly transfer

them to an ice bath to stop the cooking process.

- **Dry and Pack**: Pat the mushrooms dry with a clean towel. Spread them out on a baking sheet and freeze them individually to prevent clumping. Once frozen, transfer them to airtight freezer bags or containers.

Drying

Drying is another excellent preservation method, particularly for mushrooms like shiitake and porcini, which rehydrate well:

- **Clean and Slice**: Clean the mushrooms and slice them thinly.
- **Drying Method**: Use a food dehydrator, oven, or air-dry method to remove moisture.
- **Dehydrator**: Set your dehydrator to around 110°F (43°C) and dry for 4-8 hours.
- **Oven**: Set your oven to the lowest temperature and dry the mushrooms on a

baking sheet for 6-8 hours, flipping occasionally.

- **Air-Dry**: Thread the mushroom slices onto a string and hang them in a well-ventilated area away from direct sunlight. This method can take several days.
- **Storage**: Store dried mushrooms in airtight containers in a cool, dark place. They can last for months or even years.

Pickling

Pickling mushrooms adds a unique flavor and extends their shelf life:

- **Clean and Slice:** Clean the mushrooms and slice them if desired.
- **Prepare Brine:** Make a brine with vinegar, water, salt, sugar, and your choice of spices.
- **Cook and Jar:** Simmer the mushrooms in the brine for 5-10 minutes. Transfer them to sterilized jars, fill with brine, and seal tightly. Store in the refrigerator.

Tips for Optimal Storage

- **Avoid Moisture:** Moisture is the enemy of fresh mushrooms. Always keep them dry and avoid washing them before storage.
- **Check Regularly**: Inspect your stored mushrooms regularly for any signs of spoilage, such as discoloration or off odors.
- **Use Promptly**: Fresh mushrooms are best used within a week of harvesting. For longer storage, consider freezing, drying, or pickling.

Proper storage is key to enjoying your mushrooms at their best. By following these tips, you'll ensure your mushrooms stay fresh and delicious for as long as possible.

CHAPTER 9

Utilizing Your Harvest

Uses of Mushrooms

Mushrooms are incredibly versatile and can be used in a variety of ways to enhance your meals, improve your health, and even support sustainable living. In this section, I'll guide you through the many uses of mushrooms, showcasing their culinary, medicinal, and environmental benefits. Let's explore how you can make the most of your mushroom harvest.

Culinary Uses

Mushrooms are a culinary delight, adding unique flavors, textures, and nutrients to dishes. Here are some popular ways to use them in your kitchen:

Cooking and Baking

- ***Sautéing***: Sauté mushrooms in a bit of oil or butter with garlic and herbs. They make

a delicious addition to pasta, rice, and meat dishes.

- ***Roasting***: Toss mushrooms with olive oil, salt, and pepper, then roast them in the oven until they're crispy and golden. Roasted mushrooms can be added to salads, grain bowls, or served as a side dish.
- ***Soups and Stews***: Add mushrooms to soups and stews for a rich, umami flavor. They work well in both creamy and broth-based recipes.
- ***Stir-Fries***: Include mushrooms in your favorite stir-fry recipes. They pair well with a variety of vegetables, proteins, and sauces.

- ***Stuffed Mushrooms***: Large mushroom caps, like portobellos, can be stuffed with fillings such as cheese, breadcrumbs, and herbs for a tasty appetizer or main dish.

Stuffed Mushrooms

- ***Pizzas and Flatbreads***: Top pizzas and flatbreads with sliced mushrooms for an earthy flavor that compliments cheese and other toppings.

- ***Baking***: Incorporate mushrooms into savory baked goods like quiches, pies, and tarts. They add depth of flavor and a hearty texture.

Preserving

- **Pickling**: Pickle mushrooms in a vinegar brine with spices for a tangy treat that can be enjoyed on sandwiches, salads, or as a snack.
- **Drying**: Dry mushrooms to preserve them for later use. Rehydrate dried mushrooms in water or broth before adding them to recipes.
- **Freezing**: Freeze cooked mushrooms to have on hand for quick meals. Blanch them first to maintain their texture and flavor.

Medicinal Uses of Mushrooms

Mushrooms have been valued for their medicinal properties for thousands of years. Various cultures around the world have harnessed the healing power of fungi to support health and wellness. In this section, I'll delve into the fascinating world of medicinal mushrooms, exploring their health benefits and how you can incorporate them into your routine to enhance your well-being.

1. Immune System Support

One of the most well-known benefits of medicinal mushrooms is their ability to boost the immune system. Here are some key mushrooms that excel in this area:

Reishi (Ganoderma lucidum)

- **Benefits**: Reishi mushrooms are often referred to as the "Mushroom of Immortality" due to their powerful immune-boosting properties. They contain beta-glucans, which enhance the activity of white blood cells, critical for fighting infections.
- **How to Use**: Reishi is typically consumed as a tea, tincture, or in capsule form. For tea, simmer dried reishi slices in water for at least 30 minutes.

Turkey Tail (Trametes versicolor)

- **Benefits**: Turkey Tail mushrooms are rich in polysaccharide-K (PSK) and polysaccharopeptide (PSP), compounds known to strengthen the immune system and have potential anti-cancer properties.
- **How to Use**: Turkey Tail can be made into a tea by simmering the dried

mushroom in water. It is also available in powdered form and as capsules or extracts.

2. Anti-Inflammatory and Antioxidant Properties

Chronic inflammation is linked to various health conditions, including heart disease, diabetes, and cancer. Medicinal mushrooms can help reduce inflammation and oxidative stress in the body:

Chaga (Inonotus obliquus)

- **Benefits:** Chaga mushrooms are rich in antioxidants, which combat free radicals and reduce oxidative stress. They also have anti-inflammatory properties that can help reduce chronic inflammation.
- **How to Use**: Chaga is commonly consumed as a tea. To prepare, grind the dried mushroom and simmer in water for at least an hour. It's also available as a powder or tincture.

Lion's Mane (Hericium erinaceus)

- **Benefits**: Lion's Mane mushrooms contain bioactive compounds that have neuroprotective and anti-inflammatory effects. They support brain health, enhance cognitive function, and may help reduce symptoms of anxiety and depression.
- **How to Use**: Lion's Mane can be consumed in various forms, including as a tea, tincture, or in capsule form. It can also be added to soups and stews.

3. Digestive Health

Mushrooms can also support digestive health by promoting a healthy gut microbiome and improving nutrient absorption:

Maitake (Grifola frondosa)

- **Benefits**: Maitake mushrooms are known for their ability to regulate blood sugar levels and improve insulin sensitivity, which is beneficial for digestive health. They also support gut health by promoting the growth of beneficial bacteria.

- **How to Use:** Maitake mushrooms can be added to soups, stews, and stir-fries. They are also available in supplement form, including powders and capsules.

Cordyceps (Cordyceps militaris)

- **Benefits:** Cordyceps mushrooms are renowned for their ability to enhance energy levels and athletic performance. They support respiratory health and improve oxygen utilization, which can aid digestion.

- **How to Use:** Cordyceps can be consumed as a tea, in capsule form, or added to smoothies and other beverages.

4. Cancer Support

- **Turkey Tail**: Studies have shown that PSK, a compound in Turkey Tail, can enhance the immune system's ability to fight cancer cells. It's used as an adjunct therapy in cancer treatment in some countries.

- **Reishi**: Reishi mushrooms may help inhibit the growth of cancer cells and reduce the side effects of chemotherapy.

5. Cognitive Health

- **Lion's Mane**: This mushroom is particularly noted for its neuroprotective properties. It stimulates the production of nerve growth factor (NGF), which is essential for the growth and maintenance of neurons, potentially improving memory and cognitive function.

Cardiovascular Health

- **Shiitake (Lentinula edodes)**: Shiitake mushrooms contain compounds like eritadenine and beta-glucans that help lower cholesterol levels and support cardiovascular health.
- **How to Use**: Shiitake mushrooms can be used in cooking, such as in soups, stir-

fries, and as a meat substitute. They are also available in supplement form.

How to Incorporate Medicinal Mushrooms into Your Routine

Integrating medicinal mushrooms into your daily routine can be easy and enjoyable. Here are some practical tips:

Teas and Tinctures

- Preparation: Many medicinal mushrooms are available as dried slices or powders. To make a tea, simmer the mushrooms in water for at least 30 minutes. Tinctures can be added to water, tea, or taken directly.
- Daily Use: Start with small doses and gradually increase based on your body's response.

Supplements

- **Forms**: Capsules, powders, and extracts are convenient ways to consume medicinal mushrooms. Follow the recommended dosage on the product label.
- **Combining**: Some supplements combine multiple mushrooms for a broader range of benefits.

Culinary Applications

- **Cooking**: Add fresh or dried mushrooms to your favorite recipes. Soups, stews, stir-fries, and even smoothies can benefit from the addition of medicinal mushrooms.
- **Flavor Enhancer**: Use mushroom powders as a seasoning to enhance the umami flavor of dishes.

Medicinal mushrooms offer a plethora of health benefits, from boosting the immune system and reducing inflammation to supporting cognitive and digestive health. By incorporating them into your daily routine through teas, supplements, and culinary uses, you can harness the healing power of these remarkable fungi.

Here's a quick summary of what we've covered:

Immune Support: Reishi and Turkey Tail enhance immune function.
Anti-Inflammatory and Antioxidant: Chaga and Lion's Mane reduce inflammation and oxidative stress.
Digestive Health: Maitake and Cordyceps support gut health and energy levels.

Value-Added Products and Processing

Environmental Uses of Mushrooms

Mushrooms are not just used for cooking and medicine alone; they also play a significant role in environmental sustainability. Fungi are crucial in natural ecosystems, contributing to soil health, waste decomposition, and even pollution cleanup. In this section, I'll guide you through the various environmental uses of mushrooms and how they can contribute to a healthier planet.

1. Mycoremediation: Cleaning Up Pollutants

One of the most remarkable environmental applications of fungi is mycoremediation, the use of mushrooms to clean up contaminated environments. Here's how it works and its applications:

What is Mycoremediation?

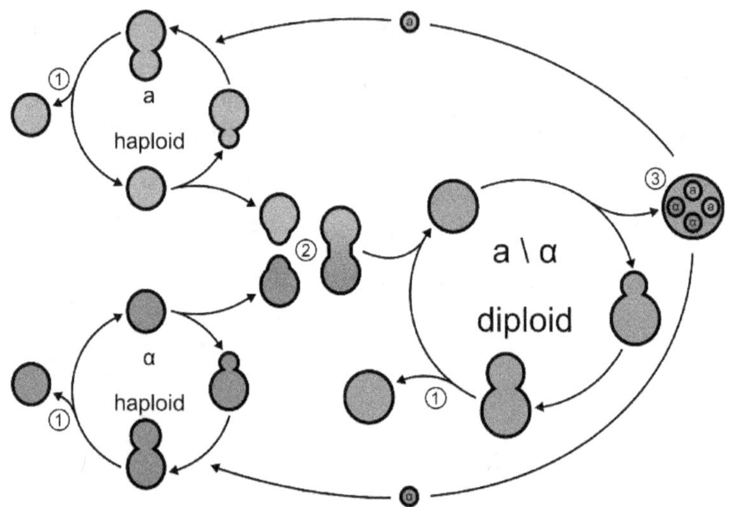

Mycoremediation leverages the natural digestive processes of fungi to break down pollutants and toxins in the environment. Fungi produce enzymes that can degrade a wide range of substances, including hydrocarbons, pesticides, heavy metals, and industrial waste.

Applications of Mycoremediation

- **Oil Spill Cleanup**: Oyster mushrooms (Pleurotus ostreatus) are particularly effective at breaking down hydrocarbons found in oil spills. They can be used to treat contaminated soil and water by inoculating the area with mushroom spores or mycelium.

- **Pesticide Degradation**: Certain fungi can degrade harmful pesticides, making agricultural land safer for future use. This is particularly useful for organic farming practices where soil health is paramount.
- **Heavy Metal Absorption**: Fungi like turkey tail (Trametes versicolor) and shiitake (Lentinula edodes) can absorb heavy metals from contaminated soil and water, reducing environmental toxicity.

How to Implement Mycoremediation

- **Inoculation**: Introduce mushroom spores or mycelium to the contaminated area. This can be done by mixing mycelium with a substrate like straw or sawdust and spreading it over the affected site.

- **Monitoring**: Regularly monitor the site to assess the effectiveness of the fungi in breaking down contaminants. Adjust the fungal species or application method as needed.

2. Soil Enrichment: Enhancing Soil Health

Mushrooms play a vital role in maintaining and improving soil health through their symbiotic relationships with plants and their ability to decompose organic matter. Here's how fungi contribute to soil enrichment:

Mycorrhizal Fungi

Mycorrhizal fungi form symbiotic relationships with the roots of plants. These fungi enhance the plant's ability to absorb water and nutrients, particularly phosphorus, which is often limited in soil.

- **Benefits to Plants**: Improved nutrient uptake, enhanced drought resistance, and increased disease resistance.

- **Benefits to Soil**: Improved soil structure, increased organic matter, and enhanced microbial activity.

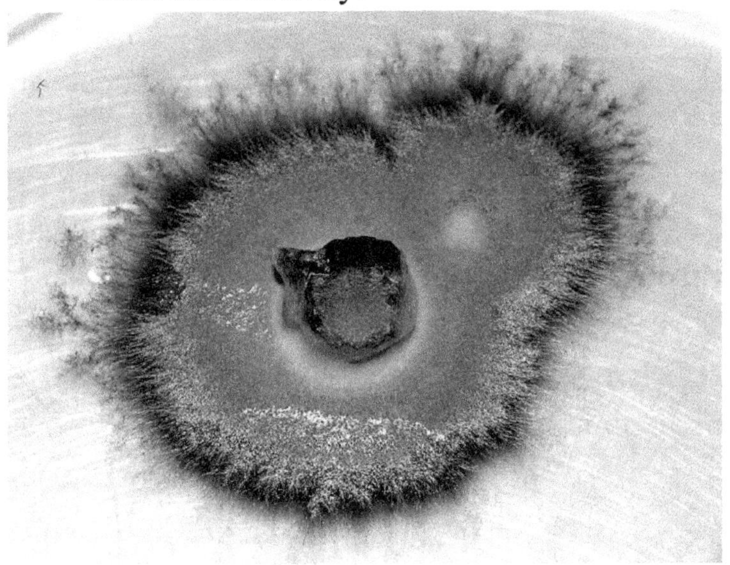

Saprophytic Fungi

Saprophytic fungi, such as oyster and shiitake mushrooms, decompose organic matter, returning essential nutrients to the soil.

- **Composting**: Adding mushroom compost to your garden enriches the soil with nutrients and beneficial microorganisms. Mushroom compost can be made by inoculating a compost pile with mushroom spores or mycelium.

- **Soil Amendment**: Use spent mushroom substrate (the material left after mushroom cultivation) as a soil amendment to improve soil fertility and structure.

3. Waste Management: Reducing Waste through Fungi

Mushrooms can be used to manage waste effectively, reducing the environmental impact of agricultural and industrial byproducts:

Agricultural Waste Recycling

Fungi can break down agricultural waste, such as straw, wood chips, and coffee grounds, converting it into valuable compost and reducing landfill use.

- **Straw and Sawdust**: Oyster mushrooms are often grown on straw and sawdust, turning these waste materials into nutrient-rich compost.
- **Coffee Grounds**: Coffee grounds are an excellent substrate for growing mushrooms. By using them for mushroom cultivation, you can reduce waste and produce a valuable food source.

Industrial Waste Recycling

Certain fungi can decompose industrial waste, making it safer for disposal or reuse:

Textile Waste: Fungi can break down cellulose in textile waste, reducing the volume of waste and producing useful byproducts like biofuels.

Plastic Degradation: Research is ongoing into fungi that can degrade plastics, offering a potential solution to plastic pollution.

4. Sustainable Materials: Mycelium-Based Products

Mycelium, the root-like structure of fungi, is being used to create sustainable, biodegradable materials. Here's how mycelium is transforming industries:

Packaging

Mycelium-based packaging is a sustainable alternative to plastic and Styrofoam. It is biodegradable, compostable, and can be produced using agricultural waste.

- **How It's Made**: Mycelium is grown on a substrate like straw or sawdust in molds, forming the shape of the packaging material. Once the mycelium has fully colonized the substrate, it is dried to stop growth.
- **Applications**: Used for packaging electronics, furniture, and other consumer goods.

Building Materials

Mycelium can be used to create strong, lightweight, and fire-resistant building materials:

- **Mycelium Bricks**: These bricks are made by growing mycelium on agricultural waste. They are biodegradable, have good insulation properties, and are a sustainable alternative to traditional bricks.
- **Insulation Panels**: Mycelium insulation panels offer excellent thermal and acoustic insulation while being environmentally friendly.

Textiles

Researchers are exploring the use of mycelium to create sustainable textiles:

- **Mycelium Leather:** Mycelium can be used to produce a leather-like material that is biodegradable and sustainable. It is being used in fashion and upholstery as an eco-friendly alternative to animal leather.

Mushrooms are not only a vital part of our diet and medicine cabinet but also play a crucial role in environmental sustainability.

Here's a summary of their environmental uses:

Mycoremediation: Using fungi to clean up pollutants and contaminants from soil and water.
Soil Enrichment: Enhancing soil health through mycorrhizal and saprophytic fungi.
Waste Management: Reducing agricultural and industrial waste by decomposing organic matter and recycling waste materials.
Sustainable Materials: Creating biodegradable packaging, building materials, and textiles from mycelium.

By leveraging the power of fungi, we can address some of the most pressing environmental challenges and move towards a more sustainable future. Whether you're a gardener, a farmer, an environmentalist, or simply someone interested in sustainability, incorporating mushrooms into your practices can have a significant positive impact on the environment.

Walter K. Byrne

CHAPTER 10

Advanced Techniques and Innovations

Scaling Up Production

If you've been bitten by the mushroom cultivation bug and find yourself dreaming of a bigger, more bountiful harvest, then you've come to the right place. In this section, I'm going to guide you through the exciting journey of scaling up your mushroom production. Get ready to expand your operation, increase your yields, and take your mushroom-growing game to the next level!

Why Scale Up?

Before we dive into the nitty-gritty of scaling up your mushroom production, let's talk about why you might want to do it in the first place:

- **Meet Demand**: Maybe you've been selling your mushrooms at farmers' markets or to local restaurants, and demand is booming. Scaling up allows you to meet the needs of your customers and grow your business.
- **Maximize Efficiency**: With larger-scale production methods, you can streamline your processes, reduce labor costs, and increase overall efficiency.
- **Explore New Markets**: Scaling up opens doors to new opportunities, whether it's supplying grocery stores, selling online, or even exporting your mushrooms.

Assessing Your Options

Now that you're sold on the idea of scaling up, let's explore some of the options available to you:

Expanding Your Growing Space

- ***Indoor Expansion***: If you're currently growing mushrooms indoors, consider expanding your growing space by adding more grow rooms, shelves, or racks. This allows you to increase your production capacity without needing more land.
- ***Outdoor Expansion***: If you have access to outdoor space, such as a garden or unused land, consider setting up outdoor mushroom beds or building a greenhouse to grow mushrooms year-round.

Investing in Equipment

- **Upgrading Equipment:** As you scale up, you may need to invest in larger equipment such as commercial-grade incubators, sterilizers, and climate control systems to handle larger volumes of substrate and mushrooms.
- **Automation**: Explore automation options to streamline your processes and reduce

manual labor. This could include automated watering systems, conveyor belts for substrate handling, and robotic harvesters.

Optimizing Production Techniques

- **Bulk Substrate Preparation**: Instead of mixing substrate by hand, consider investing in equipment for bulk substrate preparation, such as a compost turner or substrate mixer. This allows you to prepare larger batches of substrate more efficiently.
- **Spawn Production**: If you're currently purchasing spawn from a supplier, consider producing your own spawn to reduce costs and ensure a consistent supply.
- **Planning for Growth**
  Scaling up your mushroom production isn't just about buying more equipment or expanding your growing space – it also requires careful planning and strategy.

Market Research

- **Know Your Market**: Research market demand for mushrooms in your area and identify potential sales channels, such as farmers' markets, restaurants, grocery stores, or online platforms.
- **Explore Niche Markets**: Consider specializing in specific mushroom varieties or targeting niche markets, such as gourmet restaurants, health food stores, or farm-to-table establishments.

Financial Planning

- **Budgeting**: Create a detailed budget outlining the costs involved in scaling up your operation, including equipment purchases, infrastructure upgrades, labor costs, and ongoing expenses.
- **Securing Funding**: Explore funding options such as loans, grants, or

investment partnerships to finance your expansion plans.

- **Scaling Up Gradually**: Instead of trying to scale up all at once, consider taking a gradual approach. Start by making small investments in equipment or expanding your growing space incrementally to minimize risk and ensure a smooth transition.

Scaling up your mushroom production can be an exciting and rewarding journey, but it also comes with its challenges. Remember to stay flexible, adapt to changing circumstances, and most importantly, enjoy the process! By embracing growth and continually refining your techniques, you'll be well on your way to a thriving mushroom operation that delights customers and sustains your passion for fungi.

Experimenting with Advanced Cultivation Methods

If you've mastered the basics and are ready to take your mushroom cultivation skills to the next level, you're in the right place. In this section, we'll explore some advanced cultivation methods that can help you optimize your yields, experiment with new techniques, and maybe even discover a new favorite way to grow mushrooms. Let's dive in and get those creative spores flowing!

Why Experiment with Advanced Methods?
Before we get into the details, let's talk about why you might want to try out these advanced methods:

1. **Boost Yields**: Advanced techniques can often lead to higher yields, allowing you to get more mushrooms from the same amount of substrate.
2. **Improve Quality**: These methods can help you grow mushrooms that are larger, healthier, and more consistent in quality.

3. **Enhance Efficiency**: Advanced techniques can streamline your growing process, saving you time and effort.
4. **Expand Your Knowledge**: Experimenting with new methods is a great way to learn more about mushroom cultivation and deepen your expertise.

Liquid Culture

Liquid culture is an advanced method that involves growing mycelium in a nutrient-rich liquid medium. This can lead to faster colonization times and healthier mycelium.

How to Make Liquid Culture

1. **Prepare the Medium**: Mix water with a small amount of honey, malt extract, or another sugar source to create a nutrient-rich solution. Sterilize it in a pressure cooker.
2. **Inoculate the Liquid**: Using a sterile syringe, inject mushroom spores or a

small piece of mycelium into the liquid medium.

3. **Incubate**: Store the culture at a temperature suitable for mycelium growth (usually around 70-75°F or 21-24°C). Shake the container regularly to distribute the mycelium evenly.

Once the liquid is cloudy with mycelium, use it to inoculate your substrate. This can significantly speed up the colonization process.

Grain Spawn Expansion

Grain spawn expansion involves using a small amount of colonized grain to inoculate a larger quantity of sterile grain. This method is excellent for scaling up your production efficiently.

Steps for Grain Spawn Expansion

1. **Prepare the Grain**: Soak and boil grains such as rye, wheat, or millet. Drain and sterilize them in jars or bags.
2. **Inoculate the Grain**: Add a small amount of colonized grain spawn to the sterile grains. Shake or mix the grains to distribute the mycelium.
3. **Incubate**: Store the jars or bags in a dark, warm place (around 70-75°F or 21-24°C) until the new grain is fully colonized.
4. **Repeat**: You can use some of the new colonized grain to inoculate even more grains, creating a cycle of expansion.

Monotub Method

The monotub method is a popular technique for growing mushrooms, particularly for those aiming to produce larger quantities. It involves using a single large container (monotub) to create an ideal environment for fruiting.

How to Set Up a Monotub

1. **Prepare the Tub**: Use a plastic storage container and drill holes for ventilation. Cover the holes with micropore tape or polyfill to filter contaminants.
2. **Prepare the Substrate**: Mix your chosen substrate (such as coir, vermiculite, and gypsum) and pasteurize it to kill any unwanted organisms.
3. **Layer the Tub**: Add a layer of colonized grain spawn to the bottom of the tub, followed by a layer of the prepared substrate. Continue layering until the tub is full.
4. **Incubate**: Keep the tub in a warm, dark place until the substrate is fully colonized by mycelium.
5. **Fruiting Conditions**: Once colonized, introduce the tub to fruiting conditions by increasing humidity and providing indirect light.

Cold Shock Technique

Some mushroom species, such as shiitake, benefit from a cold shock to initiate fruiting.

This method mimics natural temperature changes that signal the mushrooms to start growing.

How to Cold Shock

1. **Complete Colonization**: Ensure your substrate is fully colonized.
2. **Lower Temperature**: Place the colonized substrate in a refrigerator or cold area (around 40°F or 4°C) for 24-48 hours.
3. **Return to Normal Conditions**: After the cold shock, move the substrate back to fruiting conditions with the appropriate temperature and humidity.

Experimenting with advanced cultivation methods can be incredibly rewarding. Not only will you potentially increase your yields and improve the quality of your mushrooms, but you'll also gain a deeper understanding of the fascinating world of fungi. Don't be afraid to try new techniques, make mistakes, and learn from them. Every experiment is a step toward becoming a more skilled and knowledgeable mushroom cultivator.

So, roll up your sleeves, gather your supplies, and let's get experimenting. Who knows? You might just discover the next big thing in mushroom cultivation.

CONCLUSION

Congratulations on making it to the end of this comprehensive guide on mushroom cultivation! As we've explored the fascinating world of fungi together, I hope you've found this journey as enlightening and exciting as I have. Let's take a moment to summarize what we've covered and reflect on the key takeaways from each section of this book.

We started with an introduction to the enchanting world of mushrooms, learning about their unique biology and the basics of their life cycle. Understanding these fundamentals is crucial for any successful cultivator, as it sets the foundation for everything that follows.

Next, we discussed how to select the right mushroom species for your cultivation goals, whether you're interested in the reliable button mushroom, the flavorful shiitake, the versatile oyster, the robust portobello, the delicate enoki, or the medicinal lion's mane. Each species has its own quirks and requirements, and choosing the right one is a critical first step.

Setting up your cultivation space was our next topic. Whether you're working indoors with a controlled environment or taking advantage of outdoor spaces, creating the perfect conditions for your mushrooms is essential. We covered the necessary equipment and materials, from basic tools to more specialized gear, ensuring you're well-prepared for every stage of growth.

Growing and Harvesting

We delved into the specifics of the mushroom life cycle, emphasizing the importance of each growth phase. From inoculation techniques to substrate preparation, you now have a solid understanding of how to create an ideal environment for your mycelium to thrive.

When it comes to harvesting, timing is everything. Knowing when to harvest and using proper techniques ensures you get the best quality mushrooms, whether for your personal use or for selling to eager customers. We also explored how to store your harvest to maintain freshness and maximize shelf life.

By Becoming more comfortable with basic cultivation, experimenting with advanced methods can open new doors. From liquid cultures to monotubs, and even cold shock techniques, these methods can enhance your yields, improve mushroom quality, and make your process more efficient.

Scaling up production is an exciting step for those ready to take their hobby or small business to the next level. With detailed planning, market research, and a gradual approach to expansion, you can successfully grow your operation while maintaining quality and sustainability.

The journey doesn't end with the harvest. Mushrooms offer a plethora of opportunities beyond fresh produce. We explored various value-added products and processing methods, such as drying, powdering, and pickling, which can add diversity to your product offerings and extend the usability of your mushrooms.

Mushrooms also have incredible medicinal and environmental benefits. From immune-boosting properties to their role in bioremediation, the potential uses of mushrooms are vast and impressive. Whether you're looking to enhance your health or contribute to environmental sustainability, mushrooms have a role to play.

No journey is without its hurdles. We covered common issues in mushroom cultivation, from contamination to pests, and provided strategies for overcoming these challenges. With the right knowledge and preparation, you can turn potential setbacks into learning experiences, ensuring your cultivation efforts remain fruitful.

Final Tips

Finally, we shared some last-minute tips to help you succeed. From maintaining a clean workspace to continuously learning and experimenting, these tips are designed to keep you on the path to becoming a master cultivator.

Mushroom cultivation is a rewarding and continually evolving practice. Whether you're a hobbyist enjoying a fruitful pastime, a small business owner expanding your horizons, or an environmental enthusiast looking to make a difference, the world of mushrooms offers endless opportunities.

Remember, the key to success is patience, curiosity, and a willingness to learn. Every batch of mushrooms, every experiment, and every challenge encountered is a step forward in your journey.

Thank you for allowing me to guide you through this fascinating world. I hope this book has provided you with the knowledge and inspiration to pursue your mushroom cultivation dreams. May your grow rooms be ever bountiful, your harvests plentiful, and your passion for mushrooms ever-growing.

Happy cultivating!

APPENDIX

Agar: A gelatinous substance derived from seaweed, used as a culture medium for growing fungi.

Autoclave: A device that uses steam under pressure to sterilize equipment and substrates.

Colonization: The process by which mycelium spreads throughout the substrate.

Fruiting Body: The reproductive structure of a mushroom, which produces spores.

Mycelium: The vegetative part of a fungus, consisting of a network of fine white filaments (hyphae).

Pasteurization: The process of heat-treating substrates to kill pathogens without completely sterilizing them.

Spawn: A carrier material that contains mycelium, used to inoculate the substrate.

Substrate: The material on which mycelium grows, providing nutrients and support.

Inoculation: The process of introducing spawn into a substrate.

B. Equipment and Materials List
Basic Equipment

- Pressure cooker or autoclave
- Mason jars or spawn bags
- Gloves and face mask for hygiene
- Alcohol for sterilization
- Petri dishes (for agar work)
- Syringes (for liquid culture)

Advanced Equipment

- Food dehydrator (for drying mushrooms)
- Grain mixer or compost turner
- Commercial incubators
- Climate control systems
- Automation tools (e.g., automated watering systems)

Materials

- Grain (rye, wheat, millet)
- Substrates (coir, vermiculite, gypsum)
- Nutrient additives (malt extract, honey)
- Spawn (grain, sawdust)
- Micropore tape or polyfill (for ventilation)

C. Common Mushroom Species and Their Requirements

1. Button Mushroom (Agaricus bisporus)

- Ideal Substrate: Compost
- Temperature: 65-75°F (18-24°C)

- Humidity: 85-95%
- Light: Low light
-

2. Shiitake Mushroom (Lentinula edodes)

- Ideal Substrate: Hardwood sawdust or logs
- Temperature: 55-70°F (13-21°C)
- Humidity: 85-90%
- Light: Moderate light

3. Oyster Mushroom (Pleurotus ostreatus)

- Ideal Substrate: Straw or sawdust
- Temperature: 60-75°F (15-24°C)
- Humidity: 80-95%
- Light: Bright indirect light

4. Portobello Mushroom (Agaricus bisporus)

- Ideal Substrate: Compost
- Temperature: 65-75°F (18-24°C)
- Humidity: 85-95%
- Light: Low light

5. Enoki Mushroom (Flammulina velutipes)

- Ideal Substrate: Sawdust or straw
- Temperature: 45-60°F (7-15°C)
- Humidity: 85-95%
- Light: Low light

6. Lion's Mane Mushroom (Hericium erinaceus)

- Ideal Substrate: Hardwood sawdust
- Temperature: 65-75°F (18-24°C)
- Humidity: 85-95%
- Light: Indirect light

D. Recipes for Value-Added Products

Dried Mushrooms
- Preparation: Clean and slice mushrooms uniformly.
- Drying Method: Use a food dehydrator set to 125°F (52°C) or air dry in a well-ventilated area.

- Storage: Store in an airtight container in a cool, dry place.

Mushroom Powder

Preparation: Dry mushrooms thoroughly.

Grinding: Use a spice grinder or blender to create a fine powder.

Storage: Store in an airtight container, away from light and moisture.

Pickled Mushrooms

Preparation: Clean and trim mushrooms.

Brine: Heat vinegar, water, sugar, and salt until dissolved. Add spices as desired.

Pickling: Pour brine over mushrooms in sterilized jars. Seal and refrigerate.

E. Troubleshooting Common Issues

Contamination

- Signs: Unusual colors, foul odors, slimy texture.

- Prevention: Maintain strict hygiene, sterilize equipment and substrates, use clean spawn.

Poor Fruiting

Causes: Incorrect humidity, insufficient light, contaminated substrate.

Solutions: Adjust humidity levels, provide appropriate lighting, ensure substrate is clean and healthy.

Pests

Signs: Presence of insects, chewed mycelium or mushrooms.

Prevention: Keep the growing area clean, use screens to keep out pests, regularly inspect your grow area.

F. Resources and Further Reading

Books

1. "Growing Gourmet and Medicinal Mushrooms" by Paul Stamets

2. "The Mushroom Cultivator" by Paul Stamets and J.S. Chilton
3. "Mycelium Running" by Paul Stamets

Websites

http://www.mushroomgrowersassociation.com
https://fungi.com
http://www.shroomery.org

Online Communities

- Reddit's r/MushroomGrowers
- The Shroomery Forums
- Facebook groups dedicated to mushroom cultivation

G. Final Tips and Best Practices

- Stay Hygienic: Always work in a clean environment and use sterilized tools and materials.
- Keep Learning: The field of mushroom cultivation is always evolving. Stay

updated with new research and techniques.

- Document Your Process: Keep a journal of your cultivation process, noting what works and what doesn't. This will help you improve over time.
- Network with Others: Join online forums and local groups to share experiences and learn from other growers.
- Be Patient: Mushroom cultivation can be unpredictable. Patience and persistence are key to success.